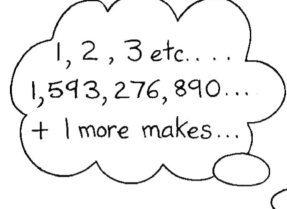

Honest weights and measures

● Mathematical concepts

Weights; capacities; use of simple measuring instruments; comparing, ordering objects according to weight or capacity.

● Numeracy Document links

Measures, shape and space
- Reception: use language such as ... heavier or lighter ...
- Year 1: compare two ... masses or capacities by direct comparison
- Year 2: ... measure and compare ... masses and capacities
- Year 3, 4, 5: ... measure ... mass or capacity

● Key Christian belief

Honesty in daily life.

● From the Bible

Amos 8:4-5 (Paraphrase)

Listen to this, you people who are cruel to the poor, who can't wait for the special days to be over so that you can sell your goods again. All you want to do is overcharge and cheat using scales that have been changed so they don't weigh properly.

Deuteronomy 25:13-16 (NIV)

Do not have two differing weights in your bag · one heavy, one light. Do not have two differing measures in your house · one large, one small. You must have accurate and honest weights and measures ... For the LORD your God detests *(hates)* anyone who does these things, anyone who deals dishonestly.

● You will need

Liquid measures
Weights and scales (different types if possible)
1 litre carton of milk
1 kg bag of sugar
Other items to weigh or measure
Sticky tack
1 penny

● Introduction

Note: *Italics* = instructions for teachers

Measure and weigh various items checking that the weight/volume on the packet is accurate. Teachers will need to assist younger pupils with the weighing and measuring. Older pupils can do this themselves, using both kilograms and litres. (Extra items can be brought in for older pupils.)

Tell the pupils about the work of the Trading Standards Office and how it is wrong to sell something advertised with a particular weight/volume when it actually contains less. It is against the law, and shops could get into trouble for this. Trading Standards Officers regularly check weights and measures to make sure they are accurate. This can be turned into a drama about the visit of the Trading Standards Officer.

*Ask pupils if they can think of a way in which dishonest people might cheat customers using weights and measures. Show them how people used to cheat by using sticky tack to stick a penny under one pan of the scales (see illustration). Talk about what this does to the customer. **Older pupils** can dramatise a scene where a shop-keeper cheats a customer by adding something to the bottom of the scales. Alternatively, they can think of other ways in which customers may be cheated. **Note:** please stress that this assembly is about a problem that occurred in the past. Today shops are regularly inspected.*

● Core material

Cheating is not a new problem. The Bible tells us that some shop-keepers deliberately cheated their customers by altering the weight so that the customer paid the full price but got less for their money. *Read the material from the Bible.* **Younger pupils** *only need the material from Amos.* Not only was this against the law in the Bible, it was seen as an insult to God. Christians believe God is true and just (fair), therefore anything dishonest is against his character. They also believe that he created all people and anything that hurts a person (such as cheating) hurts God.

● Prayer/Reflection

Ask pupils to look at the scales as a focus as you read the prayer below. Pupils can join in with the line, "Who cares? God does" if this is appropriate. Alternative: ask pupils to think about other ways honesty can be practised in daily life.

Overcharging customers:
Who cares? God does.
Cheating the poor:
Who cares? God does.
Altering the weights:
Who cares? God does.
Thank you, Father, that you care about the ordinary things:
Weights and measures;
Cheating and honesty
and how people live their lives.

● Music suggestions

'Jesus I know you live', *Big Blue Planet*, edited by J. Jarvis (Stainer and Bell and Methodist Church Division of Education and Youth, 1995)

'God cares for you and me', *Children's Praise*, compiled by P. Burt, P. Horrobin and G. Leavers (Marshall Pickering, 1991)

ASSEMBLIES THAT COUNT

22 Broadly Christian Assemblies for Primary Schools linked to the Mathematics Curriculum

Margaret Cooling and Catherine O'Connell
in conjunction with Maths Year 2000

CONTENTS

MATHS YEAR 2000

INTRODUCTION

At The Stapleford Centre, we had the idea of producing an assembly book relating to maths. In 1999, the National Numeracy Strategy for England was published and this was the spur we needed. When Maths Year 2000 was launched, we talked together and they were keen to support our proposed project. *Assemblies that Count* is the result!

Christian assemblies

These assemblies demonstrate the link between maths and Christianity and is <u>one</u> example of how maths and religion relate. Other faiths make different links which can also be explored.

The maths link

The assemblies in this book all relate to maths in some way. An assembly may:

- explore a mathematical idea - insofar as it relates to a religious concept or story
- reinforce mathematical language
- explore one aspect of a famous Christian mathematician
- explore the symbolic use of numbers and shapes.

The assemblies may be used to stimulate learning in maths. They may sum up or reinforce work done in the classroom. The assemblies are not, however, an occasion for initial maths teaching and should in no way replace maths. The emphasis should be on worship, and maths as a route to worship.

Why maths and worship?

The link between maths and worship may strike some teachers as unusual, but, in former ages this would have been considered perfectly natural. Today, we tend to divide knowledge into religious and secular. No such division existed in the Middle Ages. Professional mathematicians were often clergy in Medieval times and numbers had a religious, symbolic value. (The Bible itself uses number in this way.) Don't worry if it feels strange to link maths to religion, this is just the result of a change in our culture. This book merely returns to an earlier tradition.

What is the link between maths and Christianity?

Christians believe in a Creator God whose work can be discovered in a ordered and beautiful universe. Maths is part of that pattern and order. In earlier times maths and theology were seen as different ways of exploring God's world. Mathematicians such as Isaac Newton wrote many commentaries on the Bible as well as writing books on maths and science. Maths moved the mathematician Johannes Kepler to awe and worship.

Incorporating the assemblies into themes

Each assembly can be used individually, as part of a series of maths assemblies, or as part of another series of assemblies. For example:

- the assemblies on Kepler and Newton can be used as part of a wider series on famous people
- the assemblies on the cross and the halo can be used as part of a series on symbols
- the assemblies on tithing and inequality can be used as part of a Harvest series.

Photocopying

The illustrations in this book may be photocopied (single copies only) for use in the assembly. This permission extends to making one acetate for the overhead projector or an enlarged copy on paper.

Pupil participation

There are plenty of opportunities for pupils to take part in assemblies: pupils can read the biblical material, take part in maths activities, read poems and prayers. If it is a whole school assembly, small numbers of pupils can participate at the front of the hall and demonstrate to the rest of the school. Class assemblies allow a greater degree of pupil participation. Teachers will need to adapt the material according to the size of the assembly.

Assemblies/Act of Worship/Religious Observance

The word 'assemblies' is used in this book to refer to the act of worship, as this is the term in popular usage. Officially, however, the word 'assembly' denotes the notices and the administrative detail. The act of worship/religious observance is the religious part of the gathering.

Respecting the pupils' integrity

Assemblies should be appropriate to the pupils and to the faith of their families. There are several ways of making worship appropriate.

- Involvement in worship should be sensitive to a pupil's family background. Pupils should not be encouraged to join in things which would be inappropriate. Choose people to participate in activities with care. Sometimes alternatives are provided.

- Christian material should be introduced using phrases such as "Christians believe", or "Today we are looking at a story from the Bible which is very important to Christians". Assent should not be assumed. This approach protects the integrity of the pupil and the teacher, whilst enabling a full and accurate presentation of Christianity.

- Pupils should be aware that a variety of responses are acceptable, as long as they are respectful. Responses might vary between appreciating that what has been said is important to Christians, through to adoration of God. Worship should not (and cannot) be compelled. This means allowing pupils the freedom not to join in with certain activities, but to listen respectfully instead.

Health and Safety

All activities should be conducted with health and safety considerations in mind. Teachers are referred to their school's Health and Safety document.

HOW TO USE THIS BOOK

Younger pupils/older pupils/instruction for teachers
The assemblies are aimed at pupils aged 5-11. Teachers should read the **whole** assembly in preparation. Where no age group is suggested, the material is meant for all pupils. Some words may need replacing/explaining for younger pupils.

Covering the complete age range
No assembly adequately covers a seven year age range (and an even wider ability range). However, each assembly contains material for all ages, although each assembly has a different target age. If an assembly is targeted at 7-11 year olds, there will be plenty to do for younger pupils and some material within their understanding. If teachers have just infants or just juniors they will need to select from the material provided.

Italics
Material in italics usually indicates instructions for teachers.

THE STRUCTURE OF EACH PAGE

Each page has a set structure to make it easy to follow and contains the following components:

Mathematical concepts
These are the general concepts that relate to the assembly. Teachers who are not using the English Numeracy Document should look here for links to their own maths documents.

Numeracy Document links
The assemblies are all cross referenced to *The National Numeracy Strategy for England (1999)* but the concepts chosen for this assembly book are basic ones such as shape, counting, money and weight.

Key Christian belief
This is the Christian theme explored by the assembly.

From the Bible
This consists of a passage from the Bible, often paraphrased. When a Bible passage is quoted without being paraphrased, difficult words are followed by simple alternatives in italics and brackets. Indications are given in the body of the assembly to show where the biblical material is to be used.

You will need
Items needed for the assembly are listed under this heading. These items should be collected beforehand, though time can be saved by keeping basic items in an assembly box.

Scissors
Felt-tipped pen
Sellotape and glue
Sticky tack
Paper and card

Pupils can help to make the visual aids, or they can bring in items, as part of their participation.

Introduction
This introduces the idea or subject of the assembly. This section often includes activities in which the pupils can participate. It creates a link between human experience and the religious idea in the core material.

Core Material
This section is usually where the religious concept is developed, exploring the link between human experience and the religious material.

Prayer/Reflection
Each assembly contains a prayer or reflection.

Prayers are addressed directly to God. In some prayers God is addressed as 'Father', 'Lord' or 'God'. Teachers may wish to change the way in which God is addressed in a particular prayer, but a suitable substitute should be used, bearing in mind the context. Prayers can be introduced with phrases such as, "I am going to read a Christian Prayer", or, "Listen quietly while the prayer is read. Those who wish to can join in with saying 'Amen'." Some prayers involve participation, and others can be read by pupils. Teachers should choose pupils with care for these activities. Pupils should also feel free to listen respectfully without participating.

Reflections are not addressed to God; they are for thoughtful reflection. Pupils do not have to share their thoughts, though some may wish to do so. Reflections need bringing to a close. When praying, the 'Amen' tells you that the prayer has come to an end. Create your own way of ending a reflection so that pupils know when it is finished.

If the prayer/reflection is considered unsuitable for your school, it can be replaced by a time of thinking, with a focus such as an object or a piece of music.

Music suggestions
Several songs are suggested for each assembly. If the suggested songs for the assemblies are not appropriate for your school, more general songs can be substituted.

The second page
This page often contains an illustration which can be enlarged and photocopied or put on an acetate. Sometimes it contains extra material, music or a poem.

Infinity

● Mathematical concepts
Number sequences; large numbers; infinity

● Numeracy Document links
Counting and recognising numbers
- Reception: say and use number names in order in familiar contexts; recognise numerals 1 to 9

Numbers and the number system
- Year 1: read ... numerals from 0 to at least 20
- Year 2: describe and extend simple number sequences; read ... whole numbers to at least 100
- Year 3: read ... whole numbers to at least 1000
- Year 4: read and write whole numbers ... into thousands
- Year 5: read and write whole numbers. (See *'Examples'*: thousand, million)

● Key Christian belief
God is eternal. God's love never ends.

● From the Bible
Psalm 136:1-3 (NIV)
Give thanks to the LORD, for he is good. His love <u>endures</u> *(goes on)* for ever.
Give thanks to the God of gods. His love <u>endures</u> *(goes on)* for ever.
Give thanks to the Lord of lords: His love <u>endures</u> *(goes on)* for ever.

● You will need
Black board/flip chart/OHP or a long roll of wallpaper
Pen/chalk

● Introduction
Note: *Italics = instructions for teachers*
Write 1, 2, 3 on the board (flip chart etc.) and ask pupils to supply the next number. How many numbers can they give in sequence? How long would the numbers go on if we kept adding more? (This looks best on a long roll of wallpaper with pupils holding up the roll around the room displaying the long sequence of numbers.) For **younger pupils**, *use a shorter sequence of numbers, introducing the idea of numbers following on from each other and going on and on. Ask* **older pupils** *to suggest the largest numbers they can. Explain very large numbers: a million (1,000,000 – a thousand thousands), a billion (1,000,000,000 – a thousand millions) and a trillion (1,000,000,000,000 – a million millions). Show how they are written.* Even when we reach a trillion, we could still go on counting. *Introduce the term 'infinity'. 'Infinity' means that things just go on.*

● Core material
The teacher should read the poem to **younger pupils. Older pupils** *can read the poem themselves.*

God Is Still Making Up Numbers · Steve Turner

> God is still making up numbers
> For numbers just go on and on ...
> Just when God thinks he has finished
> God knows he can always add 1.

When we wrote our numbers, however long the number line got, they still went on. No one has ever come to the end of numbers, they just go on and on *(to infinity, for* **older pupils***)*. The fact that numbers do not end reminds Christians that God does not end · they believe he goes on forever and that his love never ends. *Read the material from the Bible.* Maths acts as a reminder of the Christian belief that God and his love go on for ever. Christians believe God was there before the world was made, and he will still be there at the end of time. He was always there in the past and will always be there in the future. This means people need never be alone. God will always be present.

● Prayer/Reflection
Ask pupils to suggest things that end. For example the school day will end, it will not go on for ever. Make a list of the pupils' suggestions. If appropriate, add the repeating line, "But numbers go on forever and so does God" between each line. Pupils can join in with saying this refrain.

The alphabet starts with A and ends with Z.
The day starts with breakfast and ends with sleep.
A book starts at the beginning and ends on the last page.
A football match starts with a whistle and ends with winning or losing.
Thank you, Father, that your love never ends
but goes on for ever, like numbers.

Alternative: use the first four lines of the prayer and then ask pupils to think about the good things in life that we would want to go on forever: love, peace etc.

● Music suggestions
'Jesus' love is very wonderful', *Come and Praise Beginning*, compiled by G. Marshall-Taylor and D. Coombes (BBC, 1996)
'He'll be there', *Songs for every assembly*, by M. and H. Johnson (Out of the Ark Music, 1998)
'Jesus, Jesus, here I am', *Jump up if you're wearing red!*, compiled by The National Society (The National Society and Church House Publishing, 1996)
'God was there', *Junior Praise 2*, compiled by P. Burt, P. Horrobin and G. Leavers (Marshall Pickering, 1992)

Tithing

● Mathematical concepts
Ordinal numbers; fractions; percentages; decimals; equivalence of fractions, percentages, decimals

● Numeracy Document links
Counting and recognising numbers
- Reception: count reliably up to ten everyday objects
- Reception: begin to understand and use ordinal numbers

Numbers and the number system
- Year 1: ordinal numbers
- Year 1, 2, 3: understand and use the vocabulary of comparing and ordering numbers
- Year 3: recognise unit fractions such as ... $^1/_{10}$
- Year 4: begin to use ideas of simple proportion: ... 'one in every ... '; understand decimal notation and place value for tenths ... , and use it in context
- Year 5: use decimal notation for tenths ... ; relate fractions to decimal representations
- Year 6: express simple fractions such as ... tenths ... as percentages

● Key Christian belief
Giving to God/others

● From the Bible
Deuteronomy 14:22 (NIV)
Be sure to set aside a tenth *(Give God 1 item in every 10)* of all that your fields produce each year.

● You will need
Groups of 10 things: apples, sweets, pens etc
10 coins, either 1p coins, 10p coins or £1 coins
Sticky tack

● Introduction
Note: *Italics* = instructions for teachers
Mix up the groups of ten items. **Younger pupils** *can sort the mixed up items into groups of ten. These items can be held up by pupils standing in lines. Pupils can count how many there are of each item (ten). As they stand in a line, ordinal numbers (first, second, third etc.) can be used to label each item. Ask who has the tenth item of each group.*

Older pupils *can sort the mixed items into groups of ten and arrange themselves as above but different questions can be asked of each group:*

How many people would have to sit down if $^1/_{10}$ of your group had to be seated?
How many people would have to sit down if 0.1 of your group had to be seated?
How many people would have to sit down if 10% of your group had to be seated?
If a whole class stood up, how many would have to sit down if $^1/_{10}$ (10%, 0.1) had to be seated?

● Core material
Read the material from the Bible. In the Bible, one tenth (1 in 10) of everything a person earned or produced was 'given to God'. That means it was used to help those who had no means of supporting themselves and were in need. In Bible times, it was given to the priests and to the poor because the priests had no land to grow their own food. Later, it was given to support the local church and the poor.

These gifts had a special name; they were called TITHES. Farmers gave their corn and fruit. Families gave their money and what they grew. For example, if a family had ten pence the tenth penny went 'to God'. If a family had ten bags of corn, the tenth bag went 'to God'. The people would take their gifts to the local place of worship (it would be like taking it to a church today).

*Younger pupils can demonstrate this with the sweets/apples/ pens/coins. If ten sweets are held up by pupils, nine can be kept but the tenth one would have been 'given to God' (for those in need). Repeat this with other items as necessary. **Older pupils** can work out the tithe as above but also work out the tithe on various modern incomes using decimals, fractions or percentages.*

This law about giving was part of British law for many years. If you look at maps today you can often find places with the word 'tithe' (or the older spelling, 'tythe') in them. *Show the place names.* These are places where the tithe barns *(show picture)* were built to collect the tithes from the people. There are many tithe barns still in existence. Giving one tenth 'to God'/the poor is no longer law but many Christians carry on this practice.

Note: *This assembly can be used at Harvest time or it could be linked to an appeal (Blue Peter etc.). Matthew 6:21 could also be used as extra biblical material.*

● Prayer/Reflection
Ask pupils to count to ten before you say each line, then think quietly about it. Alternative: think about ways in which we make giving to others (not just in money) part of daily life rather than something we do when we feel moved.

1, 2, 3, 4, 5, 6, 7, 8, 9, 10.
One penny in every ten for love.
1, 2, 3, 4, 5, 6, 7, 8, 9, 10.
One penny in every ten for justice.
1, 2, 3, 4, 5, 6, 7, 8, 9, 10.
One penny in every ten for the poor.
1, 2, 3, 4, 5, 6, 7, 8, 9, 10.
One penny in every ten for God.

● Music suggestions
'I'm giving', *Children's Praise*, compiled by P. Burt, P. Horrobin and G. Leavers (Marshall Pickering, 1991)
'Jesus, you gave everything for me', *Kidsource*, compiled by A. Price (Kevin Mayhew, 1999)

Tytherington (Gloucestershire, Somerset, Wiltshire)

Tytherleigh (Devon)

Tytherton Lucas (Wiltshire)

Tythegston (Mid-Glamorgan)

Tythby (Nottinghamshire)

Tithe Green (Nottinghamshire)

A Tithe barn

The Celtic Cross

● **Mathematical concepts**

Horizontal, vertical; 2-D shapes and their properties: circle

● **Numeracy Document links**

Measures, shape and space:

- Reception: Begin to name … flat shapes such as a circle …
- Year 1: Use everyday language to describe features of familiar … 2-D shapes
- Year 2: Sort shapes and describe some of their features
- Year 4: recognise simple examples of horizontal and vertical lines

● **Key Christian belief**

The circle as a symbol of God and his love which goes on forever. The cross as a symbol of love.

● **Note:** *Italics = instructions for teachers. This material makes three assemblies. The Celtic cross is made up of two symbols (a symbol is a sign which evokes a response or feeling and has a complex meaning). The first two assemblies explore the separate symbols, the third assembly explores the meaning of the combined symbols which make the Celtic cross.*

● **From the Bible**

Assembly 1: The circle · *Psalm 90:2 (Paraphrase)*

Before the mountains were created, you were there, God. Before the earth was made, you existed. For always and forever you are God.

Assembly 2: The cross · *Luke 23:33-34 (Paraphrase)*

They led Jesus away and crucified him … Jesus said, "Father forgive them, they don't know what they are doing."

● **You will need**

Assembly 1: The circle · an enlarged version of the circle on paper or acetate. A range of circular shapes. Coins

Assembly 2: The cross · an enlarged version of the cross on paper or acetate

Assembly 3: The Celtic cross · an enlarged copy of the Celtic cross on paper or acetate

● **Introduction**

Assembly 1: The circle. *Play I-spy looking for circular shapes in the room.* What have all circles got in common? *(Ask **older pupils** to define a circle.) Ask pupils to hold up the circular shapes, and trace their fingers around the edge.* Circles have no beginning and no end.

Assembly 2: The cross. *All pupils can describe the shape of a cross and play I-spy looking for cross shapes around the room (window panes etc.).* Different things make a cross shape: birds when they fly, a sword. *This can be demonstrated by drawing a*

*simple cross shape then drawing a bird shape/sword etc. over the top in another colour. Ask pupils for their suggestions of other things that make a cross shape. **Older pupils** can explore the horizontal (explain) and vertical (explain) structure of the cross symbol.*

Assembly 3: The Celtic cross. *Recap over the previous introductions. Explain that today they are going to look at a symbol that contains both the cross and the circle.*

● **Core material**

Assembly 1: The circle. *Show the circle.* The circle reminds Christians of God because it never ends. *Read Psalm 90:2.* Christians believe that God was there before the world began, and he will still be there long after it has ended. *Explore different similes involving circles to express this Christian idea. Example. God's love is like a coin that keeps on rolling or a world that keeps on turning. Put the similes together to form an instant poem.*

Assembly 2: The cross. *Show the cross.* This shape reminds Christians of Jesus' love. Jesus died on a cross and even when dying forgave his enemies who killed him. *Read Luke 23:33-34.* Christians also believe he rose again. Death and hatred had not won. Love and life had won. Christians believe that Jesus took all the hatred and wrong and came out still loving and living. The cross became a reminder of Jesus' love and his defeat of death. *Draw a horizontal line.* This line looks like arms open to welcome everybody. *('Hands' can be drawn on the ends of the line.) Draw a vertical line.* This line points upwards to God. *(Add an arrow point.)* Together the two lines make a cross, a Christian symbol of God's love for the whole world.

Assembly 3: The Celtic cross. *Show the Celtic cross.* The Celtic cross contains a circle and a cross. *Recap over the meaning of both symbols.* Together the cross and the circle make one symbol that reminds Christians of God always being there and Jesus' love. *Show the cross and the circle and place one over the other. Use the biblical material from the previous assemblies.*

● **Prayer/Reflection**

Prayers and reflections can be found on page 11.

Alternative: listen to the words of the songs (Music suggestions) reflectively and create signs or use sign language to express them.

● **Music suggestions**

'God has put a circle round us', *Big Blue Planet*, edited by J. Jarvis (Stainer and Bell and Methodist Church Division of Education and Youth, 1995)

'Love will never come to an end', *Complete Come and Praise*, compiled by G. Marshall-Taylor (BBC, 1990)

'Magic penny', *Alleluya!*, compiled by D. Gadsby and J. Hogarth (A. & C. Black, 1980)

The Celtic cross

The circle

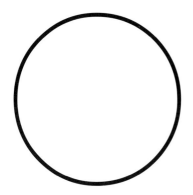

The cross

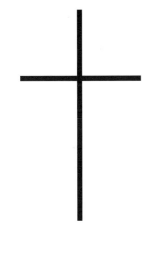

Prayer/Reflection

Assembly 1: The circle
(Read the reflection as pupils 'draw' a circle on their hands with a finger).

The ball spins round,
its shape has no beginning, no end.
God goes on forever.
The world turns in space,
its shape has no beginning, no end.
God goes on forever.
The coin goes on rolling,
its shape has no beginning, no end.
God goes on forever.

Assembly 2: The Cross
Pupils can 'draw' the shape in the air or on their hand (with their fingers).

Just two lines:
one says 'welcome', one points to 'God'.
Together they make a cross.
Together they speak of love.

Assembly 3: The Celtic cross
Circles can be made with the finger and thumb.

Circles speak of always, crosses speak of love.
Circles say, 'forever', crosses say, 'forgive'.
Circles go on turning, saying, 'God is here'.
Crosses say, 'love conquers, there is no need to fear'.

The square halo

● Mathematical concepts
2-D shapes and their properties: squares

● Numeracy Document links
Measures, shape and space
- Reception: begin to name flat shapes such as ... square
- Year 1: use everyday language to describe features of familiar ... 2-D shapes
- Year 2: Sort shapes and describe some of their features
- Year 3: Classify and describe ... 2-D shapes ... , referring to properties such as ... number of sides/edges and vertices, whether sides/edges are the same length, whether or not angles are right angles
- Year 5: recognise properties of rectangles

● Key Christian belief
Sainthood/ordinary Christians

● From the Bible
Ephesians 1:1-2 (NIV)
... To the <u>saints</u> *(believers or Christians)* in Ephesus, the faithful in Christ Jesus: Grace and peace to you from God our Father and the Lord Jesus Christ.

● You will need
Some tinsel or silver/gold paper (or use page 13)
Square objects and objects of other shapes
A bag
An enlarged version of the illustration
Ruler and protractor (optional)

● Introduction
Note: *Italics* = instructions for teachers
*Play I-spy on square objects in the room. Place some square objects and other shapes in a bag. Ask pupils to pull them out one by one and say whether they are square or not, giving a reason for their answer. Ask them what makes a square a square. (For **older pupils**, it has four equal sides and four right angles. They can measure the sides and angles.)*

● Core material
Make a halo for yourself or for a pupil using tinsel/paper. Ask who has worn one of these in a nativity play and ask what it stands for. Explain that artists sometimes paint a circle of light around some people's heads (show illustration). As an alternative cut the halo provided (see instructions) and place on the OHP to create a halo of light, under which pupils can stand. This circle of light is called a halo. A halo is a symbol *(page 10)* used to show that someone is very special, e.g. Jesus, Mary or an angel may be shown with a halo. Saints are also shown with haloes.

A saint is recognised as a special person who has lived an outstanding Christian life or died for their faith. Some of these saints are well-known, some of you may even be named after them:

St Catherine	St Paul
St Peter	St Andrew
St Margaret	St Stephen
St Mary	St Elizabeth
St Michael	St John
St Paula	St Joan

Here is one story about a recognised saint *(see the story of Saint Lawrence page 13)*.

In the Bible, however, the word 'saint' is used of **all** Christians. 'Saint' just means someone who is committed to God, a Christian. *Read the material from the Bible.* When artists wanted to show one of these ordinary Christians who was still alive they couldn't use a round halo because people would get muddled and think they were a special saint *(someone who has died or who has lead an outstanding Christian life)*. Artists got round this problem by using a square halo for ordinary, living Christians. *Tell the story of the MAF pilots (see page 13)*.

● Prayer/Reflection
Pupils can perform actions as the prayer/reflection is read. The tinsel halo can also be held up as a focus. Alternative: ask pupils to think of ordinary people who have made a difference to the world/other people's lives and quietly say thank you for them.

Circular haloes tell of saints, special people. *(Use a finger and thumb to create a circle.)*
Square haloes tell of ordinary living Christians.
(Use two fingers and thumbs to create a square.)
No-one really has a halo, circular or square.
Thank you, Father, for the special people,
who have stood firm for their faith.
Thank you also for the ordinary saints,
the people who try to live out Jesus' teaching today.

● Music suggestions
'In our work and in our play', *Children's Praise*, compiled by P. Burt, P. Horrobin and G. Leavers (Marshall Pickering, 1991)
'Signs of Jesus', *Rejoice 1*, complied by A. White, A. Byrne and C. Malone (HarperCollins Religious, 1993)

Note: *pictures of haloes can be found on the internet on art sites.*

A saint with a round halo

An ordinary person with a square halo

Enlarge this section.
Cut out the shaded areas
and secure the centres
with sellotape.
Place this section
on the OHP to create
haloes of light.

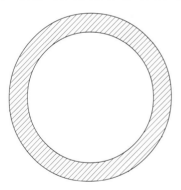

The story of Saint Lawrence (died 598)

When Lawrence lived, it was dangerous to be a Christian, but Lawrence was a saint with a sense of humour. The leader of the Christians was arrested by the Romans, but before he was taken away, he gave Lawrence all the books and treasures of the Church. Lawrence hid the books to keep them safe, but he sold all the treasures and gave the money to the poor. Some time later the Roman ruler demanded that Lawrence hand over all the Church's treasures. Lawrence agreed to do this but said he would need a few days to collect them together. Lawrence collected all the poor and down and outs he could find and presented them to the ruler saying, "These are the Church's treasures; the poor are of great value to Christ." As you can imagine the ruler was not pleased, and eventually Lawrence was sentenced to be killed by burning. Even facing death it is said he showed his sense of humour, saying, "I think I'm done on this side - why not turn me over?"

MAF Pilots: ordinary 'saints'

MAF stands for Mission Aviation Fellowship. For 50 years MAF pilots have been flying tiny planes into some of the world's most remote places, places where ambulances and doctors cannot reach. Tough but small aircraft are used because they have to be able to land on rough ground - no smooth runways for these pilots. Every four minutes a MAF plane takes off to help someone. Pilots fly eye surgeons and their teams to remote areas of Africa. This enables surgeons to perform eye operations. Such a team can save the sight of up to 30 people a day. These pilots do not make the news but they are modern day 'saints'.

The Fellowship of the Least Coin

● Mathematical concepts
Recognise coins, money; least, smallest

● Numeracy Document links
Solving problems:
- Reception: problems involving ... money; sort coins ...
- Year 1: recognise coins of different values
- Year 2, 3: use £.p notation

Measures, shape and space
- Reception: put objects in order of size

● Key Christian belief
Justice, peace, reconciliation

● From the Bible
Luke 21:1-4 (NIV)
As he looked up, Jesus saw the rich putting their gifts into the temple treasury. He also saw a poor widow put in two very small copper coins. "I tell you the truth," he said, "this poor widow has put in more than all the others. All these people gave their gifts out of their wealth; but she out of her poverty put in all she had to live on."

● You will need
A variety of coins including 1p, 10p and £1 coins.
Option for *older pupils:* coins from other countries
Items you could buy for 1p
A plate or tin

● Introduction
Note: *Italics* = instructions for teachers
Place the British coins on a table and ask pupils to find the 'least coin' (the coin with the least value). Using this coin ask them what they could buy for 1p. Display the items that can be purchased for 1p. A scene in a sweet shop could be dramatised.

Older pupils can locate the 'least coin' in other currencies using the coins provided.

● Core material
Read the story from the Bible and/or dramatise it. The widow gave two very small coins, the smallest available, the 'least coins'. Jesus praised the woman for giving these because they were given with love and they really cost her a lot. They were not just left-overs she could spare. Although the coins the woman gave were worth very little, far less than a 1p piece, the love that came with them made them valuable to God.

Older pupils: Explain that the two coins were Jewish lepta, small bronze coins, the smallest imaginable. It took two of these to make a Roman quadrans which was the smallest Roman coin. When Jesus lived, both Jewish and Roman coins were in use (like pounds and Euros).

All pupils: In 1956, Mrs Shanti Solomon started 'The Fellowship of the Least Coin'. The women who belonged to this organisation realised that there was much wrong with the world. There was injustice (unfairness), war, and hatred. They decided to pray for justice, peace and reconciliation (love, forgiveness). Every time they pray, each member gives the least coin in her own currency and the money is used to fund projects to further justice, peace and reconciliation. *(This story can be dramatised.)*

The coins the women give are very small, just like the coins the widow gave in the story, but like the widows' coins they come with love and prayer. Although the monetary value is small, they are highly valuable in another way. With many women praying and donating their least coin with every prayer, the money mounts up and can be used to change people's lives.

● Prayer/Reflection
You will need three coins (1p, 10p, £1) and a plate. Ask pupils to think about a situation that needs peace and justice as they hear the coin land on the plate. Alternative: just use the 'something to think about' sections.

One penny given with love, is worth more to God than a hundred given with pride.

Drop 1p on the plate
(Something to think about: the rich nations of the world get most of the world's money.)

Ten pence given with care, is worth more that a thousand given lightly.

Drop 10p on the plate
(Something to think about: the rich nations of the world get most of the world's health care.)

One pound given with prayer, is worth more than a million given to impress.

Drop £1 on the plate
(Something to think about: the rich nations of the world get most of the world's food.)

For God can take the smallest gift and make it do great things.

● Music suggestions
'Magic penny', *Alleluya!*, compiled by D. Gadsby and J. Hogarth (A. & C. Black, 1980)
'It's the little things', *Junior Praise 2*, compiled by P. Burt, P. Horrobin and G. Leavers (Marshall Pickering, 1992)

The widow gives her small coins

Kepler's snowflakes

● Mathematical concepts
Reflective symmetry; rotational symmetry

● Numeracy Document links
Measures, shape and space
- Reception: talk about, recognise ... patterns: e.g. ... symmetrical patterns in the environment
- Year 1: make symmetrical patterns
- Year 2: begin to recognise line symmetry
- Year 3: identify ... lines of symmetry ...
- Year 6: rotational symmetry

● Key Christian belief
God as designer

● From the Bible
Psalm 19:1-4 (Paraphrase)
The universe clearly shows how clever God is. No words are heard but the message goes round the world.

● You will need
Enlarged copy of the snowflake on acetate or paper
Paper and scissors (see diagram)

● Introduction
Note: *Italics* = instructions for teachers
Cut some snow crystal shapes by folding and cutting the paper as shown. Keep talking while you cut, asking pupils to guess what you might be making. Explain that snow crystals are frozen water (vapour) that makes lovely patterns, and the crystals join together to form snowflakes.

● Core material
Display the snow crystal shapes or place them on the OHP. Ask pupils what they notice about them. **Younger pupils:** *both sides look the same; they have six points.* **Older pupils:** *they display line and rotational symmetry and have 6 'points' or vertices.* **Older pupils** *can explore the rotational symmetry, if appropriate.* Each snowflake is unique. Each has its own design.

This pattern in snow crystals and snowflakes was noticed by a famous mathematician called Johannes Kepler who lived between 1571 and 1630. When Kepler was a young man he wanted to be a minister (like a vicar/priest). He went to university to train as a minister and while he was there he studied mathematics. Kepler became so good at maths that he was persuaded to become a mathematician instead of a minister, but he never lost his faith in God. When Kepler worked on the snowflake he saw it as discovering the patterns that the Creator God had built into nature. Mathematics could help him to discover God's great designs. *Read the material from the Bible.* In 1600 Kepler wrote about the snowflake and its symmetry. For Kepler, Maths led him to praise God. **Older pupils:** *Read the poem by Clive Sansom.* **Younger pupils:** *Read the story of Sam.*

Sam the Snow Crystal that lost his Flake
Sam was a snow crystal. He was a very beautiful snow crystal, in fact there was no one else quite like him! His six points were covered in lacy ice patterns that made him look like a frozen star. *(Three pupils stand one behind the other and hold out their arms to form a snow crystal shape.)* Sam, however, was not a happy snow crystal; he was all alone. It had all started in the middle of the night. He had floated to earth through the freezing air, and as he did so, other snow crystals joined him until he was part of a large snow flake. The other snow crystals held onto his six points: there were Cyril and Sandra, Sean and Samantha, Steve and Sophie. *(Six pupils each hold an arm/point.)* They had landed by a big rock and the wind had blown them under its edge, but as the sun rose, its rays peeped in under the rock. First Cyril melted, then Sandra. Sean and Samantha melted a little later and finally Steve and Sophie. (*The pupils let go two at a time.)* Now, he was the only one left and what use was a snow crystal that had lost his flake? Sam felt worried; he could feel his points beginning to melt. *(The six arms/points wiggle their fingers.)* "This is it," he thought. "Not long now and I will be nothing but water." But Sam was wrong! The sun went down, it got cold again and the wind blew more snow under the rock. "Mind if we join you?" said Susan and Simon the snow crystals. "Of course not," said Sam, holding out two points. *(Two pupils each hold an arm/ point.)*

● Prayer/Reflection
Kepler discovered the pattern and shape of snowflakes. We also know that every snowflake is made up of snow crystals - sometimes as many as 100. Each crystal has 6 sides or points. As far as we know, each one is different. The same is true of snowflakes; each is six sided or has six points and as far as we know each one is different. Close your eyes and imagine how many snowflakes fall in one snowfall. Now imagine how much snow falls all around the world. The number of different snowflakes is unimaginable! *Place the snowflake on the OHP as you read Kepler's comment - paraphrase for younger pupils. Alternative: omit the prayer.*

"I thank thee O Lord our Creator, that thou hast permitted me to look at the beauty in thy work of creation. I exalt thee in the works of thy hands." (Kepler in *Harmony of the World*)

● Music suggestions
'All things bright and beautiful', *Complete Come and Praise*, compiled by G. Marshall-Taylor (BBC, 1990)
'See how the snowflakes are falling', *Someone's Singing, Lord*, by B. Harrop (A. & C. Black, 1992)

How to cut a snow crystal shape

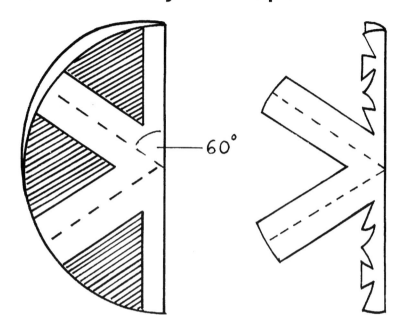

60°

Cut each arm of the snowflake in the same pattern (for rotational symmetry).

Snowflakes · Clive Sansom

And did you know
That every flake of snow
That forms so high
In the winter sky
And falls so far,
Is a bright six-pointed star?
Each crystal grows
A flower as perfect as a rose.
Lace could never make
The patterns of a flake.
No brooch
Of figured silver could approach
Its delicate craftsmanship. And think:
Each pattern is distinct.
Of all the snowflakes floating there ·
The million million in the air ·
None is the same. Each star
Is newly forged, as faces are,
Shaped to its own design
Like yours and mine.
And yet . . . each one
Melts when its flight is done;
Holds frozen loveliness
A moment, even less;
Suspends itself in time ·
And passes like a rhyme.

A snow crystal

Sir Isaac Newton

● Mathematical concepts
Money (£2 coin); position vocabulary (front, back, edge); year (date)

● Numeracy Document links
Solving problems
- Reception: begin to understand the vocabulary related to money; sort coins including … £2
- Year 1: recognise coins of different values
- Year 2, 3: use £.p notation

Measures, shape and space
- Reception: use everyday words to describe position
- Year 3: calendar and dates

Reinforcing mathematical vocabulary
- money, coin, front, back, edge

● Key Christian belief
Humility, acknowledging others, not boasting

● From the Bible
1 Corinthians 13:4-7 (NIV)
Love is patient, love is kind. It does not envy, it does not boast, it is not proud. It is not rude, it is not self-seeking, it is not easily angered, it keeps no record of wrongs. Love does not delight in evil but rejoices with the truth. It always protects, always trusts, always hopes, <u>always perseveres</u> *(never gives up)*.

Philippians 2:2-4 (Paraphrase)
Live together in peace by showing love for each other. Be one in your thinking. Don't be jealous or boastful, but be humble and think of others as more important than yourselves. Care about them as much as you care about yourselves.

● You will need
1p, 10p, £1, and £2 coins
Enlargements of the drawings
Items for a 'shop'

● Introduction
Note: *Italics = instructions for teachers*
Younger pupils: *Dramatise a shop scene where **younger pupils** can buy items using different coins.* There are lots of coins. How do we know which coin to use when we shop? There is information on coins to help us. *Show the 1p, 10p and £1 coins and ask **younger pupils** to find the following:*

front
back   This can be repeated by older pupils on a £2 coin
edge

The back of the coin tells us what type of coin it is and its value: e.g. 1p, 10p, £1, £2. *Ask pupils to find the value of a variety of coins by looking on the back of each coin. They can make suggestions concerning what each coin will buy.* The £2 gives us extra information.

Front: the Queen, the Queen's name, some Latin which translated reads: Elizabeth II, by the grace of God, Queen, Defender of the Faith.

Back: the date; the value of the coin; a symbol:
  1999 coin: a Rugby ball for the year of the Rugby World Cup
  1997, 1998, 2000 coin: three sets of wheels representing:
    (i)   the explosion of industrial development (cogs, gears and wheels);
    (ii) the computer age (computer chips);
    (iii) the Internet.

Edge: motto · quotation by Sir Isaac Newton 'Standing on the shoulders of giants'.

Older pupils *can look for these pieces of information for the teacher and the drawings can be enlarged and put on acetates/ large sheets of paper.*

Note: *new designs for the back of £2 coins may be issued.*

● Core material
Sir Isaac Newton was a brilliant mathematician and, like Kepler before him, he was a Christian. Newton made many discoveries in both maths and science. He worked on gravity, the telescope, light and colour, and explained how tides and comets worked. People often called him a genius but Newton said that he 'stood on the shoulders of giants'. He did not mean that he literally stood on giants' shoulders! He meant that many people like Kepler had done work before him and he developed their work further. They had 'giant' brains. He merely finished what they started. In doing this Newton displayed an attitude recommended in the Bible. *Read the two passages from the Bible. Emphasise not boasting and humility.*

● Prayer/Reflection
Show the front, back and edge of a £2 coin for the relevant parts of the prayer. Alternative: change the prayer suggestions to thinking suggestions.
The front of the coin shows a picture of the Queen. The Bible tells people to pray for rulers, that they may be just and fair. *(Spend a few moments praying for those who rule.)*
The back shows the date, a reminder of time, a precious gift. *(Spend a few moments asking God for the wisdom to use time wisely.)*
On the edge is a motto *(read it out)*. In life we all 'stand on the shoulders of giants'. We all build on the thinking and work of those who went before us. Give us the humility, God, to recognise this.

● Music suggestions
'Let us love one another', *Children's Praise*, compiled by P. Burt, P. Horrobin and G. Leavers (Marshall Pickering, 1991)
'Jesus put this song into our hearts', *A Year of Celebration*, edited by J. Porter and J. McCrimmon (McCrimmon, 1995)

The front of a £2 coin

The back of a £2 coin

The edge/rim of a £2 coin

STANDING ON THE SHOULDERS OF GIANTS

Mathematical message

● Mathematical concepts
Weight; division (as sharing)

● Numeracy Document links
Counting and recognising numbers
- Reception: say and use the number names in order in familiar contexts

Measures, shape and space
- Year 1, 2: understand and use vocabulary related to ... mass

Calculations
- Year 2: begin to understand division as ... sharing
- Year 3: understand division

● Key Christian belief
God as Judge

● From the Bible
Story of Belshazzar, Daniel 5, retold below.

● You will need
Pan scales & weights
Cake and knife
Pens and paper

● Introduction
Note: *Italics = instructions for teachers*
1. *Talk about numbering with pupils. If we number the days in a week they go 1, 2, 3, ... , 7 etc. Seven is the last day. Do the same with a group of pupils and number them, pointing out the last pupil.*
2. *Show the pan scales and ask pupils to weigh the cake.*
3. *Take the cake and ask pupils how it could be divided.*

Make sure pupils know what the terms 'numbered', 'weighed' and 'divided' mean. Explain that today's story from the Bible includes all of these. **Note:** *this is a difficult story. Involve the **younger pupils** in these introductory activities to help them understand it.*

● Core material
*The play can be prepared before the assembly by **older pupils**. Streamers and party whistles can be used for the party and appropriate actions can be developed. The words, 'Numbered, Numbered, Weighed, Divided' can be put on the OHP or on a large sheet of paper at the appropriate point in the story.*

Narrator: King Belshazzar held a great feast. The cooks had been busy for days, as there were over a thousand guests! Everyone had plenty to eat and drink. Belshazzar looked around the hall. "How rich and powerful I am," he thought.

Belshazzar: Servants! Bring the gold and silver cups from the Temple of the Jewish God in Jerusalem! We deserve the best.

Narrator: The cups were soon brought and filled with wine and the party became very noisy.

Belshazzar: Our gods helped us to defeat the God of the Jewish people. Our gods are great gods!

Guests: *All cheer.*

Narrator: Suddenly, everyone became silent. The King dropped his cup and pointed at the wall. There, a hand was writing four words · *Numbered, Numbered, Weighed, Divided.*

Belshazzar: What do those words mean? Someone tell me what those words mean!

Narrator: The wise men were called for but none of them knew. They just shook their heads.

Queen: What about Daniel, Your Majesty? He is one of the Jews, a very wise man. He will help.

Narrator: Daniel was sent for and the king waited impatiently.

Daniel: King Belshazzar, I can tell you what these words mean, because God will tell me. You made fun of God. You used the special cups from his Temple for your own party. You said that your gods, who are only statues, are greater than he is. Listen to his message to you.

The word **numbered** means that he has looked at your life and it does not please him. Your days as king are numbered. You have reached your last day. The word **weighed** means God has 'weighed' and judged your life and found there is not enough goodness in it.

The word **divided** means God will take your Kingdom and divide it amongst others.

Work through the story picking out and explaining the following:
- *Daniel said Belshazzar's days were numbered. His time was up. He had been a bad King.*
- *Daniel said God had 'weighed' Belshazzar's life. He did not really mean that he had put Belshazzar in the scales! It is a way of saying that he had looked at the good and bad points of Belshazzar's life and the bad 'outweighed' the good.*
- *Belshazzar had a large kingdom. Daniel said it would be divided and given to someone else who could rule it better.*

Note: *the words would have been in Hebrew, the language of the Jews, as shown in the illustration.*

● Prayer/Reflection
Use the pan scales as a focus. Using paper and pens create the reflection below. Alternatively, enlarge the picture of pan scales on page 7 and write the words directly on the pans. Alternative: use the pan scales and write on paper the qualities that should be in the good 'pan' and ask pupils to think about them.

Belshazzar was 'light' on love *(write love on one of the pieces of paper and drop it into the pan),*
Light on goodness *(ibid.),*
Light on justice *(ibid.),*
Light on humility *(ibid.).*
God calls people to be 'heavy' on (have lots of) all these things.

● Music suggestions
'Let love be real', *Our Songs*, edited by Kevin Mayhew (Kevin Mayhew, 1998)
'Let us love one another', *Children's Praise*, compiled by P. Burt, P. Horrobin and G. Leavers (Marshall Pickering, 1991)

© The Stapleford Centre 2000

'Belshazzar's Feast', a sketch of a part of Rembrandt's painting

Pattern

● **Mathematical concepts**

Pattern with 2-D shapes; shapes that will tile (tessellate); 2-D shapes and their properties: hexagon

● **Numeracy Document links**

Measures, shape and space
- Reception: patterns ... in the environment
- Year 2: use the mathematical names for common 2-D shapes: ... hexagon; describe features

Solving problems
- Year 2, 3: ... recognise simple patterns and relationships

● **Key Christian belief**

God as Designer

● **From the Bible**

Romans 1:20 (Paraphrase)

From the beginning, God's wisdom and power has been seen in the things he has made.

● **You will need**

Enlarged copy of drawings provided on paper or acetate
Box of plastic shapes
Sticky tack
A transparent ruler and protractor
2kg and 50g weight
A jar of honey

● **Introduction**

Note: *Italics = instructions for teachers*

*Show the different shapes. Ask pupils to name them. Ask pupils which ones they think would fit together without gaps, using sticky tack to fix them to a board (or place on an OHP). Experiment with various shapes to show which ones fit together without gaps (introduce the word tessellate for **older pupils**) and which ones do not. You may wish to demonstrate how a hexagon is constructed for **older pupils.***

Shapes can make all sorts of patterns. Some of these patterns are found in nature. We are going to look at (regular) hexagons. *Hold up a regular hexagon, or place it on the OHP and, with the pupils, work out its properties. This can be done using a transparent ruler and protractor (**older pupils**).*

***Younger pupils**: Ask how many sides the hexagon has. Are they all the same size?*

***Older pupils**: It has six equal sides and six equal external angles at the points/vertices. **Older pupils** can come and measure the hexagon to check.*

● **Core material**

Ask which pupils like honey. Where does honey come from? We are going to trace the honey in this jar.

Bees live in places called 'hives'.
The bees produce wax.
They use the wax to make 'cells' or rooms in the shape of regular hexagons.
They join all the hexagons together to make a honeycomb.
A honeycomb is where the bees lay their eggs.
One egg is put in each cell or 'room'.
Bees collect sweet liquid from flowers called 'nectar'.
They turn the nectar into honey.
They place the honey in the cells.
People collect the honey.

If the bees made circular cells there would be gaps and the honeycomb would not be very strong. If they made triangular cells, it would not be the right shape for the eggs. Squares would be better, but the best shape of all is the regular hexagon. These fit together without any gaps and make a comfortable home for the larvae. Hexagons also make a strong structure. A honeycomb made from just 50gms of beeswax can hold 2kgs of honey! *Show the weights to pupils and invite some to feel the weight.*

The pattern (tessellation) we find in maths is repeated by bees. The bees have no rulers, and no protractors but they can still make regular hexagons. Christians often see the beautiful patterns in nature as a sign that God created the world. *Read the material from the Bible.* The cleverness of animals, the beauty in the design of the world, the wonderful patterns we see in nature, are all evidence for Christians that someone who was very clever and wise – they believe it to be God – created the world.

● **Prayer/Reflection**

Place a transparent ruler and protractor on the OHP as a focus or hold them up as you read the reflection below. Pupils can join in the lines in bold, or these can be omitted. Alternative: show a series of pictures on video of the amazing things animals can do, to evoke a sense of wonder and ask pupils to close their eyes and think about the wonderful world in which they live.

Without a ruler the bee makes a home. **Buzz, buzz.**
Without a protractor it makes a hexagon. **Buzz, buzz.**
Who told the bee it was a strong shape? **God did.**
Which maths classes did they attend? **None.**
And so the bee tells everyone how clever God is.

● **Music suggestions**

Play the 'Flight of the Bumble Bee', Rimsky Korsakov, (Polygram 4561952) for pupils to enter and leave the assembly.

'God made the colours', *Children's Praise*, compiled by P. Burt, P. Horrobin and G. Leavers (Marshall Pickering, 1991)

A hexagon

A bee

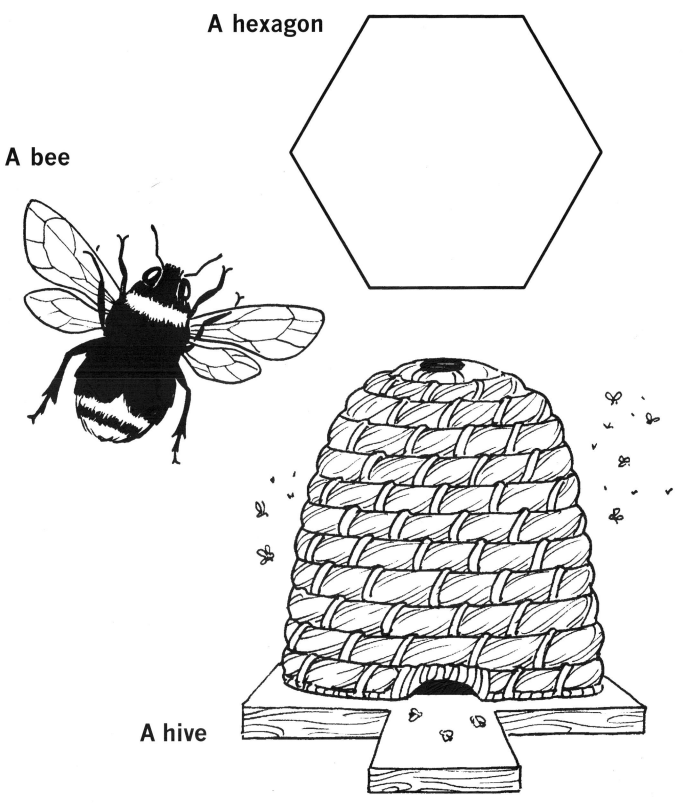

A hive

The inequality of life

● Mathematical concepts

Displaying data using pictures, pictograms, graphs; numbers greater than 1000

● Numeracy Document links

Solving problems
• Year 2: ... organising information ... in a pictogram
Handling data
• Year 3, 4: interpreting numerical data in ... graphs, e.g. a pictogram

● Key Christian belief

Justice and fairness

● From the Bible

1 Corinthians 13:1-2 (Paraphrase)
I may be good at talking, but if I have no love, my speech is nothing more than a noisy cymbal or a clanging bell. I may be good at teaching the Bible; I may have all knowledge and great faith. But if I have no love, I am nothing.

● You will need

A suitcase with some basic necessities inside:
water; food; blanket; wood; matches; tent or picture of a house.
An enlarged/acetate version of the pictogram
Ten paper plates

● Introduction

Note: *Italics = instructions for teachers*
Ask pupils to name the basic things that people need to live. Open your suitcase. Ask pupils to remove an article at a time and say why it is needed. Across the world, many people are without these basic necessities. For example, many people are without adequate food. This is not because the world does not produce enough food. Many people go to bed hungry because food is not shared out evenly.

Ask 10 pupils to hold up 10 paper plates. Imagine the 10 people represent all the people of the world, and the plates represent the food available to feed those people. If food is shared fairly, each person would have one plate of food each, but food is not shared out evenly. The rich countries of the world eat most of the world's food. It is like 3 people eating 7 platefuls of food. *(Ask three pupils to take another four plates, leaving some pupils without food.)* The rest of the world has to make do with very little. **Older pupils:** *this can be shown as a pictogram - see diagram.* This is very unfair, and many Christian organisations, such as Christian Aid, CAFOD and Tear Fund work to make the world a fairer place. It is not only food that is not fairly shared; medicine, education and water are also unevenly distributed (shared). *An example of the unfairness of the way resources are shared can be seen in the story of Angelique (page 25).*

Note: *25% of the world's population eats 70% of the world's food. The numbers have been rounded to 30 and 70.*

● Core material

We all need food and other basic items to live but there are other things we need, too. The poet Steve Turner wrote about the things we need in life. *Ask pupils to listen for the different needs mentioned in the poem. Discuss why we need love. What is 'Light from above'?*

All We Need - Steve Turner
Food in our bellies
Hats on our heads
Water to quench us
Sheets on our beds.

Teachers to teach us
Shoes on our feet
Trousers and T-shirts
Shelter and heat.

Someone to love us
Someone to love
Hope for the future
Light from above.

We need many practical things, but human beings also need to love and to be loved. *Read the material from the Bible.* Christians would say people also need God's love. Unlike food and water, God's love is evenly distributed. Christians believe God loves everyone and loving one person does not mean there is less for someone else.

● Prayer/Reflection

Hold up the plates and ask pupils to imagine their favourite food on them and read the prayer below. Alternative: ask pupils to think of one thing on their plates for which they are thankful.

We need food, but we also need someone to love us and someone to love.
Thank you, Father, that we can wake up each morning, knowing we are loved by you and that the world is full of people who need our love.

● Music suggestions

Pupils can enter and leave to 'All you need is love' by the Beatles, The Beatles 1967-1970 (Apple 0777 7970320)
'Always remember, never forget', *Big Blue Planet*, edited by J. Jarvis (Stainer and Bell and Methodist Church Division of Education and Youth, 1995)
'I may speak', *Complete Come and Praise*, compiled by G. Marshall-Taylor (BBC, 1990)

A pictogram illustrating how food is shared out in the world

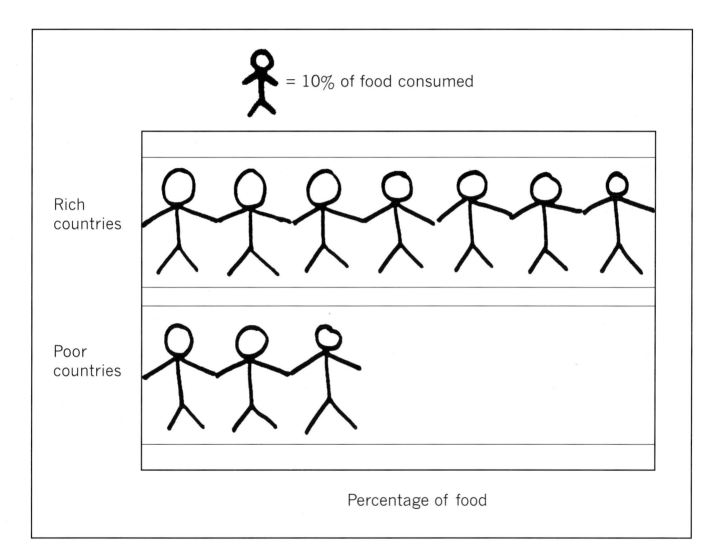

= 10% of food consumed

Rich countries

Poor countries

Percentage of food

Christian Aid

Angelique is eleven years old. She lives in Rwanda in Africa. She goes to school but has to help with lots of work at home. Her family are poor farmers. Angelique helps them grow sweet potatoes, beans and other vegetables. She grows cabbage for herself to sell in the market. With this money she buys clothes. Her mother cannot always afford them. Angelique also looks after the family's pigs and goats. The money from these helps Angelique go to school. She would like to go to secondary school in two years time but this will depend on money. It is people like Angelique and her family that are helped by organisations such Christian Aid who help people find answers to their problems.

Christmas cards

● Mathematical concepts
Recording, displaying and interpreting data using bar charts

● Numeracy Document links
Solving problems
- Year 1: organising and using data
- Year 2: ... classifying and organising information in simple ways such as ... in a block graph

Handling data
- Year 3, 4: bar charts

● Key Christian belief
That Christmas is a celebration of the birth of God's Son, Jesus.

● From the Bible
Matthew 1:18-2:23, Luke 1:26-2:20 (Paraphrase)

One day, an angel appeared to Mary - a girl who lived in the town of Nazareth. The angel told her that she would be the mother of a special baby, God's Son. She and Joseph were to call the baby 'Jesus' and they were to look after him and care for him. Everything happened as the angel said, but just before the baby was born the ruler of the country told everyone to return to the town where they had been born. Mary and Joseph had to travel to Bethlehem which was many miles away. When they arrived all the inns were full and their baby was born in a stable, for there was no room anywhere else.

On the hills around Bethlehem, some shepherds were looking after their sheep. Suddenly, a light shone down on them, and an angel spoke to them saying that God's Son had been born. The angel was joined by many others and the skies were filled with the sound of angel voices singing, "Peace on earth, goodwill to all." The shepherds hurried to the stable and found the baby, just as the angels had said. They knelt in front of the baby king and worshipped him.

Far away, some wise men spent the nights watching the stars. One night they saw a new one. "This means a great king has been born!" they said. "We must go to worship him." The star led them to Bethlehem. The wise men entered the stable and knelt before the young child. They gave him the gifts they had brought for him: gold, frankincense and myrrh.

● You will need
A range of Christmas cards showing different illustrations (reflect some of the categories on the bar chart and make sure at least one nativity scene is included)
An enlarged version of the bar chart
Paper and pens

● Introduction
Note: *Italics = instructions for teachers*

Muddle up the cards and ask pupils to sort them into sets

according to the content of the illustrations. **Younger pupils** *can help with this activity. For example, all nativity scenes together, all Father Christmas illustrations together. Pupils can also add up how many of each type there are in each set.*

Note: *For* **younger pupils** *use a small sample of about 20 cards and have only 4-6 categories (one must be the nativity). Pupils can hold up the cards and form themselves into sets.*

● Core material
Christmas is really about the birth of Jesus. For Christians this is the central event of the festival. *Read the story from the Bible.* Christmas cards do not always contain pictures of the biblical Christmas story *(refer back to the Introduction).* **Older pupils** *may want to discuss reasons for this.* **Younger pupils** *can stick the cards from their smaller sample on the wall, in vertical columns, to form an instant 'diagram'.*

Older pupils: *This is how 300 Christmas cards in a card shop in a small town were illustrated (Christmas 1999). (Pupils can have the numbers that follow on sheets of paper/card to hold up as you read out the information.)*

Animals/birds/flowers (nature)	131	Victorian scenes	8
Winter scenes	46	Church scenes, choirs	8
Christmas trees and decorations	28	Children	6
Father Christmas	22	Snowmen	6
Pretty lettering	14	Angels	4
Miscellaneous designs	12	Candles	4
Nativity scenes	11		

This could be represented as a bar chart. *Display and explain the bar chart.* Sometimes the real meaning of Christmas (it celebrates Jesus' birth) gets forgotten, but without this story, there would be no Christmas celebration.

● Prayer/Reflection
Pupils can join in the words in bold if appropriate.

In the busyness of Christmas,
Help us, Lord, to remember its real meaning.
In the bustle and the noise,
Help us to be quiet and reflect.
In the middle of parties and presents,
Help us to recall a stable two thousand years ago.

● Music suggestions
Play religious Christmas music (not secular Christmas songs) for pupils to enter and leave.

Choose any carol that reflects the Christmas story for the pupils to sing.

'Happy the day', *Children's Praise*, compiled by P. Burt, P. Horrobin and G. Leavers (Marshall Pickering, 1991)

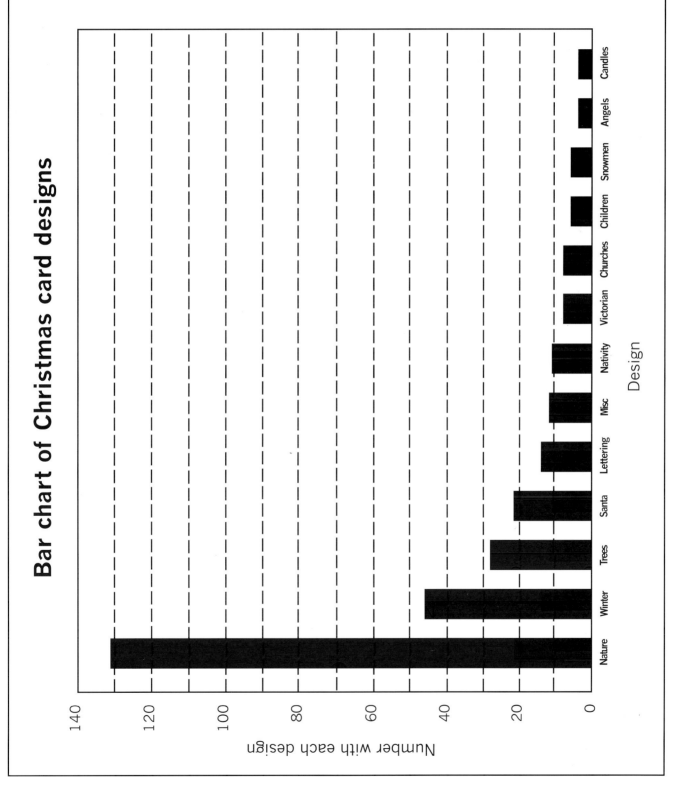

Bar chart of Christmas card designs

Number with each design

Design

Nature, Winter, Trees, Santa, Lettering, Misc, Nativity, Victorian, Churches, Children, Snowmen, Angels, Candles

Priorities

● Mathematical concepts
Ordering numbers

● Numeracy Document links
Counting and recognising numbers
- Reception: begin to understand and use ordinal numbers
Numbers and the number system
- Year 1: ordinal numbers

● Key Christian belief
Finding/making the right priorities in life. Putting God first.

● From the Bible
Matthew 6:25-34 (Paraphrase)
"Don't worry about what you will eat or drink or about what clothes you will wear. Life is more important than food and clothes. God gives food for the birds, and you are so much more important to him than birds! ... Put God first and all these other things will be given to you, for your Heavenly Father knows what you need. Don't worry about what will happen tomorrow. You have enough to worry about today."

● You will need
2 chairs
String and pegs
Card/paper and a pen

● Introduction
Note: *Italics* = instructions for teachers
Ask pupils to tell you what they do before going to bed. Write one action on each of the sheets of card/paper. Create a washing line between the two chairs. Peg the events on the line in the correct order. Number the cards: 'first', 'second', 'third' etc.

Now re-order the cards and change the numbering. What would be first now? What would be second? What would happen if you tried to do things in the wrong order? The order in which we do things doesn't always matter, but sometimes the order is very important.

● Core material
Jesus spoke about getting some things in the right order, he talked about putting God first. *Read the material from the Bible.* This does not mean that clothes and food are unimportant. Jesus said that God is even more important and should come first and that is what Christians try to do, but it is difficult. We all tend to worry about lots of things: about friends, exams, having the latest clothes etc. Christians believe that trusting in God helps people not to worry.

On three separate cards write 'God', 'food', 'clothes'. Ask pupils to put them in the order the Bible gives them and number them: 'first', 'second', 'third' etc. Explain that Jesus said that people

should look after their friendship with God first and this will help them to stop them worrying about food and clothes because they will know that God cares for them.

● Prayer/Reflection
The song on the following page can be sung reflectively as a prayer, or this reflection can be used. Explain that this is what a <u>Christian</u> *might say about God.*

God is
Number one,
the first,
the most important,
the greatest,
and the best.
The only one,
unique,
the tops.
God, the first in everything.

Alternative: Sometimes we worry about unimportant things. Think carefully about something you could do or think about, the next time you feel worried about a small thing. One strategy is to 'shrink the worry' by thinking of other more important things. You might worry about clothes, but people who know what it is like to lose their health know that <u>compared to that</u> clothes are not worth worrying about.

● Music suggestions
Learn to sing the song 'Seek ye first the Kingdom of God', if appropriate.

Older pupils may like to sing it as a round (see * for the point where the second group start).

Explain difficult words and phrases:

Kingdom of God – God's way, treating God as King, God's rule
Righteousness – God's standards that lead to right friendships
Alleluia – from the Hebrew, meaning 'praise God'

● Alternative music suggestions
'Lord, You are brilliant', *Junior Praise 2*, compiled by P. Burt, P. Horrobin and G. Leavers (Marshall Pickering, 1992)
'Mighty is our God', *Junior Praise 2*, compiled by P. Burt, P. Horrobin and G. Leavers (Marshall Pickering, 1992)

Seek ye first

Karen Lafferty
arr. Roland Fudge

'Seek Ye First' by Karen Lafferty. Copyright © 1972 Maranatha! Music.
Administered by CopyCare, P.O. Box 77, Hailsham, BN27 3EF, UK. music@copycare.com
Used by permission.

Big and small

● Mathematical concepts
Comparatives; size (length, height etc); sort and classify a set of objects according to size

● Numeracy Document links
Measures, shape and space
- Reception: language such as bigger; puts sets of objects in order of size
- Year 1, 2: understand vocabulary related to length, mass and capacity (larger, smaller, ...)

● Key Christian belief
Praise - God is worthy of praise

● From the Bible
Psalm 148:1-3, 7-12 (Paraphrase)
Praise the LORD. Praise him in heaven ... . Praise him, sun and moon, praise him all you shining stars. ... Praise the LORD from the earth, you great sea creatures and oceans, lightning and hail, snow, clouds and wind, you mountains, hills and trees, wild animals and tame ones, small creatures and flying birds. Praise him, you kings and rulers, all young men and women, old men and children.

● You will need
Big and small items and ways of measuring their size
'Praise' badges (smiley face etc.)
A paper plate ⎤
Felt pens ⎬ alternative
Scissors ⎦

● Introduction
Note: *Italics* = instructions for teachers
Mix up the big and small items and ask pupils to sort them into sets of big and small. Invite pupils to measure the items and locate the smallest and largest.

● Core material
If someone gives you 'praise', they say something really good about you. *Ask pupils what they would really like their teachers to write in their book or say about them. Show some praise badges or make one by cutting out the inside circle of a paper plate and drawing a smiling face on it.*

When Christians tell God how great he is, this is called 'praise'. They can't pin a badge on God so they tell him how great he is. The reading is about 'praise'. *Read the passage from the Bible.* In the Bible passage, the writer imagines everything, big and small, praising God: sun and moon, birds and trees. *(Ask pupils how many things they can recall.)* How could things like the stars praise God? Maybe the stars do it by shining and the birds by singing! Birds and stars do not really speak, it is a way of the writer saying that the whole earth thinks God is great.

● Prayer/Reflection
Each pupil can lift their hands to indicate something big as the first verse of the African Canticle is read. For the second verse pupils can put their finger and thumb together making a small space, indicating something small.
Note: *Teachers may wish to use visual images (video or pictures) when the canticle is read.*

An African Canticle - Desmond Tutu

All you *big* things, bless the Lord.
Mount Kilimanjaro and Lake Victoria,
The Rift Valley and the Serengeti Plain,
Fat baobabs and shady mango trees,
All eucalyptus and tamarind trees,
Bless the Lord.
Praise and extol Him for ever and ever.

All you *tiny* things, bless the Lord.
Busy black ants and hopping fleas,
Wriggling tadpoles and mosquito larvae,
Flying locusts and water drops,
Pollen dust and tsetse flies,
Millet seeds and dried Dagaa
Bless the Lord.
Praise and extol Him for ever and ever.

Infant version

All you *big* things, bless the Lord.
Mountains and lakes
Valleys and plains
Oak trees and fruit trees
Bless the Lord.
Praise Him for ever and ever.

All you *tiny* things, bless the Lord.
Busy black ants and hopping fleas,
Wriggling tadpoles and spiders,
Grasshoppers and water drops,
Bless the Lord.
Praise Him for ever and ever.

Alternative: ask pupils to think about big and small things in the world for which they feel thankful.

● Music suggestions
'God made the heavens and the earth', *Big Blue Planet*, edited by J. Jarvis (Stainer and Bell and Methodist Church Division of Education and Youth, 1995)
'Alleluya', *Alleluya!*, compiled by D. Gadsby and J. Hogarth (A. & C. Black, 1980)

Praise badges

Ant and mountain

A time for everything

● Mathematical concepts
Reading time: digital and analogue clocks

● Numeracy Document links
Measures, shape and space
- Reception: time vocabulary; begin to read o'clock time
- Year 1: read the time ... on analogue clocks
- Year 2, 3, 4: read the time ... on analogue clocks and a 12 hour digital clock
- Year 5: read the time on a 24 hour digital clock

● Key Christian belief
Life has its ups and downs but God is present in all of them.

● From the Bible
Ecclesiastes 3:1-8 extract, paraphrased. For two voices.

Everything that happens in this world has its time.
There is a time for everything.
There is a time to be born and a time to die;
A time for planting and a time for pulling up.
There is a time to kill and a time to heal;
A time for breaking and a time for building.
There is a time to cry and a time to laugh;
A time for sadness and a time for dancing.
There is a time for closeness and a time to be apart;
A time for losing, and a time for finding.
There is a time to save and a time to throw away;
A time for tearing and a time for mending.
There is a time to keep silent and a time to speak;
A time for loving and a time for hating.
There is a time to make war and a time to make peace.
There is a time for everything.

Matthew 28:20 (CEV)
I will be with you always, even until the end of the world.

● You will need
Different ways of measuring time, e.g. egg timer, candle timer, water clocks etc.

● Introduction
Note: *Italics* = instructions for teachers
People have always needed to measure time. Before clocks were invented, people used to look at the position of the sun in the sky to tell the time. They could tell if it was morning, midday or evening by the sun. For many years church bells rang when there was a service. People used the bells to work out the time and they were the 'clock' for the village or town. There are many ways of measuring time. *Demonstrate some of these with the pupils, using the different types of clock.* Each 'clock' measures time passing in some way. Clocks of various types tell us an hour has gone by or three minutes. Clocks tell us where in the day or night we are. We may look at a clock and if it says *(add appropriate time)* we know it is nearly dinner-time.

● Core material
We may be able to measure time passing, but we cannot measure what type of time it is. For example, there are sad times and happy times, and no clock can tell the difference between them. We cannot expect to be happy all the time. Neither should we expect to be sad all the time. The Bible makes it clear that life is very varied. *Read the material from Ecclesiastes.* The reading lists the different experiences that people may face – love and hate, sadness and laughter. They are all part of life even if they are not all pleasant. If we think life will always be good, we will be disappointed. If we face life knowing that life will be varied, that there will be good times and bad times, then we may be able to cope better. This advice has been set to music · *see music suggestions.* The Bible also asserts that God is with people through all these ups and down *(read the words from Matthew).*

A story – a time for sadness
Kate was miserable. That morning her sister had been taken into hospital. She knew Amy was going to be all right but she would have to spend some time in hospital. Kate missed her already · they had always done everything together. Kate walked to school with a worried expression on here face. "Cheer up Kate", said a neighbour. He hadn't heard about Amy. Kate gave him a weak smile.

"What's up with you?" shouted a friend, "You look in a right mood!" But she didn't stop to hear Kate's reply. At break-time no one talked to her. At lunch-time she ate her sandwiches alone. Just as she was finishing her last sandwich, Rachel came and sat beside her. "What's up Kate? It's not like you to be so miserable."

Kate told her about Amy. "The worst bit is that everyone expects me to look cheerful when I'm worried. It's as if I'm not allowed to be sad. I'm either told to cheer up or they avoid me."

"People find it hard to cope with sadness," explained Rachel. "I think they are frightened it's catching! They are also a bit afraid of saying the wrong thing and making you more upset. They don't mean to be unkind."

"You don't find it hard to talk to me," replied Kate. "No. My Mum had to spend a long time in hospital once, I know what it is like. Come on, let's go outside for a walk round, it's easier to talk out there."

● Prayer/Reflection
Read the words from Ecclesiastes 3:1-8 while pupils listen quietly. The words can be expressed in various ways: in dance and movement with fabric; through mime; with signing. These words have been set to music · see page 33.

● Alternative Music suggestions
'Time for everything', *Songs for every day*, by M. and H. Johnson (Out of the Ark Music, 1993)
'Song of the clock', *Tinderbox*, by S. Barratt and S. Hodge (A. & C. Black, 1983)

Turn, turn, turn

Words: Adapted from Ecclesiastes 3, vv.1-8
by Pete Seeger
Melody: Pete Seeger

To ev-'ry-thing, turn, turn, turn, There is a sea-son, turn, turn, turn, And a time for ev-'ry pur-pose un-der hea-ven.

1. A time to be born, a time to die; a time to plant, a time to reap; A time to kill, a time to heal; A time to laugh, a time to weep.

2. A time to build up, a time to break down;
    A time to dance, a time to mourn;
    A time to cast away stones,
    A time to gather stones together.
    To everything, turn . . .

·3. A time of love, a time of hate;
     A time of war, a time of peace;
     A time you may embrace,
     A time to refrain from embracing.
     To everything, turn . . .

4. A time to gain, a time to lose;
    A time to rend, a time to sew;
    A time to love, a time to hate;
    A time of peace, I swear it's not too late.
    To everything, turn . . .

Measuring time

● Mathematical concepts
Day; month; year

● Numeracy Document links
Measures, shape and space
- Reception: days
- Year 1: know the days of the week and the seasons of the year
- Year 2: order the months of the year
- Year 3: use units of time and know the relationship between them (second, minute, hour, day, week, year)

● Key Christian belief
God's gift of time

● From the Bible
Genesis 1:14-18 (GN)
Then God commanded, "Let lights appear in the sky to separate day from night and to show the time when days, years, and <u>religious festivals</u> *(special days)* begin; they will shine in the sky to give light to the earth" · and it was done. So God made the two larger lights, the sun to rule over the day and the moon to rule over the night; he also made the stars ... . And God was pleased with what he saw.

Colossians 4:5 (Paraphrase)
Make the most of the time you have.

● You will need
Cardboard sun and moon stuck on rulers or balloons
A globe (or balloon)
A clock decorated with a gift tag and ribbon
Ice-lolly · optional

● Introduction
Note: *Italics* = instructions for teachers

Explain how we use the earth, sun and moon to divide up time.

❍ A **day** is the time it takes the earth to spin round once. (***Younger pupils*** *can tell you the days of the week.) Demonstrate this with the globe. (**Older pupils**: a day is exactly 23 hours 56 minutes 4 seconds.)*

❍ A **month** is the time it takes for the moon to go round the earth. (***Younger pupils*** *can tell you the months of the year and how many there are in a year.) Demonstrate this with one pupil holding the globe and another pupil holding the moon (balloon) on a stick, walking round the 'earth'. (**Older pupils**: a month is exactly 29 days 12 hours 44 minutes 3 seconds.)*

❍ A **year** is the time it takes for the earth to go round the sun. *Demonstrate with one pupil holding the globe walking round another pupil holding the sun (balloon) on a stick. (**Older pupils**: a year is exactly 365 days 5 hours 48 minutes 46 seconds.)*

● Core material
Read the material from Genesis. In the Bible the sun, moon and stars are seen as created by God and given by him to help people mark out days and years and different times for religious festivals. The sun and moon enable people to measure time and they are probably the oldest way of telling the time. *Use the story on page 35. (Explain 'whirlpool' by referring to bathwater going down the plug-hole.)*

Christians believe that time is a gift from God. It is a present of days, months and years, but it is a present that does not last. It is like an ice-lolly on a hot day. The moment you buy an ice-lolly on a hot day it starts to melt. *(Demonstrate with lolly.)* If you just stand with it in your hand you end up with a wet hand. The moment you have a lolly you need to start licking it, or it will just melt. It will not stop melting so you might as well eat it and make the most of it. Time is a little like that. Time just keeps ticking away, we cannot stop it. The Bible has advice about using time. *Read the passage from Colossians.* Making the most of something means using it to the full, using it wisely and not wasting it.

● Prayer/Reflection
Take the clock and ask pupils to make it look like a present using the gift tag and ribbon. Display it as a focus for reflection. Alternative: omit the first line.

'To the world from God'.
The gift of time.
Every day that passes,
will not come again.
Time is a gift that cannot be hoarded.
We cannot store it,
freeze it or control it.
All we can do is use it wisely.

● Music suggestions
'It's God's Day', *Rejoice 1*, complied by A. White, A. Byrne and C. Malone (HarperCollins Religious, 1993)

'Today', *Songs for every assembly*, by M. and H. Johnson (Out of the Ark Music, 1998)

'The Clock', *Many Ways to Praise*, by S. Sayers (Kevin Mayhew, 1986)

Sun, moon and stars

A Time Story

(A fictional story set in 8th century)

Cormac and his crew of Christian monks were lost. They were sailing to the islands of Scotland to join other Christians who were working there. The waters around the Scottish islands could be dangerous. Between the islands the sea ran very fast, sometimes creating a whirlpool effect. One such place was Corryvrecken. Earlier in the day the sky had darkened · even though it was daytime · and a dark fog had rolled in. The fog was so thick that the men could only see a few feet in front of them. Without the sun to guide them they lost all sense of time. They did not know how long they had been sailing. Were they near the deadly Corryvrecken or miles away? In the silence of the fog the monks prayed:

God, you created the sun, moon and stars
out of the great darkness.
You gave them to your people, Lord,
that we might know day and night,
light and dark.
Our small ship drifts on dangerous waters.
We need your sun now, O Lord,
Hear our prayer.

The monks looked up. The fog was still thick and clinging to the ship. Eleven of the monks remained in prayer while one watched for a break in the fog. Suddenly there was a shout.

"Look overhead!"

The monks looked up. There was a small break in the fog, just a tiny patch where it looked thinner, but the patch grew in size. It was not much, but it was enough to find out the position of the sun. They could work out how long they had been sailing. They were safe!

Special days

● Mathematical concepts
Calendar; day

● Numeracy Document links
Measures, shape and space
- Reception, Year 1: days of the week; birthday; holiday
- Year 2: order the months of the year
- Year 3: use a calendar
- Year 4: use this year's calendar

● Key Christian belief
Special Holy days

● Note: *Italics = instructions for teachers.*
This assembly can be used over several days, and specific holy days can be followed up. Teachers can select from the information/activities provided.

● From the Bible
Nehemiah 8:10-11 (GN)
Now go home and have a feast. Share your food and wine with those who haven't enough. Today is holy to *(set aside for)* our LORD, so don't be sad. The joy that the LORD gives you will make you strong.

● You will need
A calendar to cut up which indicates special days (holidays etc.)
An enlarged photocopy/acetate of the illustration
Red acetate pen/felt tip pen
Scissors

● Introduction
Show the calendar and ask pupils to explain what it is. Cut up the calendar. Muddle up the months and ask 12 pupils to each select a month. Pupils can then place themselves in the correct order for the year. Once all 12 pupils are in line they can say the names of each month in order. Explain that calendars help us to order events. **Note:** *if possible choose* **younger pupils** *for this.*

Select another 12 pupils, one with a birthday in January, one with a birthday in February etc. Stand each of these 12 pupils next to the pupil holding the relevant month. By using a calendar we know that — (add name) birthday is 2 months before —— (add name).

Older pupils: *Choose a month and ask a pupil to look at the calendar page for that month and tell you the following:*
- *how many days there are in that month;*
- *any other information on the page.*

● Core material
Calendars do not only tell us the order of the months and the order of the days. They also tell us when there is a special day such as Christmas day. *Show 'December'. Ask pupils which special day for Christians happens in December. This can be*

marked on the illustration. These special religious days were called Holydays. Employers gave people time off work on these special Holydays so that they could go to church. This happened long before it was common for people to have several weeks holiday a year. Holidays were originally Holydays. Holidays are now time off work rather than a time for going to church and celebrating. *Tell the story on page 37.*

There was a tradition of celebrating in the Bible. *Read the biblical material.* Christians keep up this tradition by celebrating special events in Jesus' life or special days for praising God. Christmas, Easter, Pentecost and Ascension are holydays. *(For* **younger pupils** *only use Christmas and Easter and omit the Christian calendar which follows.)*

There are many holydays in the Christian year, not all of them are holidays (they do not get time off work for them). This is how a Christian's calendar of special holydays **might** look for one year. *(The dates change from year to year depending on the date of Easter etc.)*

January	Epiphany (the celebration of the wise men finding Jesus)
February	Candlemas (when Jesus was taken to the Temple as a baby)
March	Lent (getting ready for Easter)
April	Holy Week, Good Friday, Easter (the death and resurrection of Jesus)
May	Ascension (when Jesus said goodbye and went back to heaven)
June	Pentecost (when the Holy Spirit came)
July	Remembering followers of Jesus such as Thomas and James
August	The Transfiguration (when Jesus was shown to be someone very special)
September	Remembering Mary (Jesus' Mother)
October	Harvest (saying thank you to God for food)
November	All Saints Day (when famous Christians are remembered)
December	Christmas (the birth of Jesus)

● Prayer/Reflection
Use the illustration of the calendar as a focus as the reflection is read. Alternative: ask pupils to think about days which are special to them and what makes them special.

Thank you, Father, for special days,
For birthdays, parties, holidays and celebrations.
Remind us of the holydays days
That celebrate your goodness and Jesus' life.

● Music suggestions
'Come on and celebrate', *Junior Praise 2*, compiled by P. Burt, P. Horrobin and G. Leavers (Marshall Pickering, 1992)
'Make a joyful noise', *Kidsource*, compiled by A. Price (Kevin Mayhew, 1999)

DECEMBER

Sun	Mon	Tues	Wed	Thur	Fri	Sat
						1
2	3	4	5	6	7	8
9	10	11	12	13	14	15
16	17	18	19	20	21	22
23	24	25	26	27	28	29
30						

A Story

The Holyday Holiday
(A story set in the late 19th century)

Alice Young, like most girls of her age in the village, was a maid *(explain to pupils)*. Although she was only fourteen, she lived and worked in the big house two miles from her home. She worked for a lady called Mrs Kemp.

It was early in the morning and Alice wrapped the blankets around her, she did not want to get up. It was warm in bed. Suddenly she sat bolt upright, "It's a Holiday!" she yelled. "I don't have to go to work!" Although she did not like being a maid and living away from home, Mrs Kemp always gave her time off to go to Church on special Holy days as well as time to see her family on Sundays. "I'm better off than most," thought Alice.

Alice quickly dressed herself in her best clothes and walked the two miles home. She spent the time helping her mother and

playing with her brothers and sisters. When her father came home from work they all decided to go to church together. The family made their way to the small stone church at the top of the green. Inside the church the lights were turned down low, and they were each handed a small candle as they went in. They listened to the words of the service and sang the hymns they knew so well. The Vicar explained that this was a special service as it was a Holy day and that was why everyone had candles. He spoke about Jesus as the 'Light of the World'. The vicar lit a candle then used it to light others. Soon the whole church was full of light reflecting off the faces of the people. After the service Alice hugged her mother and said 'goodbye' to her brothers and sisters. Her father walked her to Mrs Kemp's as it was dark. They wished they still had their candles as they walked through the long lane. "Not long till Sunday." her father whispered.

"No," said Alice as she kissed him goodbye.

Not just a number

● **Mathematical concept**
Sequential numbers, large numbers

● **Numeracy Document links**
Numbers and the number system
• Year 1, 2: counting on and back in ones ...
• Year 4: million
• Year 5, 6: a thousand million (a billion)

● **Key Christian belief**
Each person matters to God

● **Note:** *Italics = instructions for teachers*
This assembly also links to citizenship.

● **From the Bible**
Isaiah 49:15-16 (GN)
"Can a woman forget her own baby and not love the child she bore? Even if a mother should forget her child, I will never forget you. ... I have written your name on the palms of my hands."

Luke 12:6-7 (NIV)
"Are not five sparrows sold for two pennies? Yet not one of them is forgotten by God. Indeed, the very hairs of your head are numbered. Don't be afraid; you are worth more than many sparrows."

● **You will need**
Wallpaper
Pens

● **Introduction**
In 1999 the world population reached six billion. This is a huge number! When we write the number in digits it looks like this: 6 000 000 000. *(Explain what a billion is for **older pupils** - one billion is one thousand million. Six billion is six thousand million.) Write six billion in numbers on a roll of wallpaper for pupils to hold up across the front of the room or copy the illustration onto an acetate. (Use **younger pupils** for this.)*

We cannot imagine such big numbers and it makes us feel very small in comparison. It can also make people feel like a number. When the 6 billion mark was reached, one baby was 'human being number 6 billion'. But that baby has a name - he/she is a person who is loved by his/her family. The family would be upset if the baby was always called 'baby 6 billion' rather than being called by his/her name. Being called by a number makes us feel less than a person.

Older pupils: We are given numbers for all sorts of things: National Insurance, Medical numbers etc. *Ask older pupils to suggest other numbers pupils are given.* Why are numbers used rather than names? Is it right to number people in this way?

Imagine your teacher stopped calling each of you by your names

and gave you all numbers and never used your name. *Demonstrate this with one infant class if **younger pupils** are present. Number the pupils sequentially and ask them to speak their numbers in sequence.* What would it be like to always be number 7?

● **Core material**
Christians believe that, to God, we are people, not just numbers. They believe he knows each person individually. *Read the material from Isaiah.* In the Bible, this is expressed by the idea of God writing people's names on his hands. That does not mean God has hands and that he literally writes names on his palms. It is picture language, a way of saying that God knows each person by name and treats each one as an individual.

Jesus also taught that God knows each person individually. *Read the material from Luke.* Jesus said that God knows and counts every hair on each person's head. *(You could ask older pupils to try to count the hairs on a person's head for one minute.) Read the poem:*

Hair 543 ... - Joan Brockelsby

Hair 54329635 fell out today.
God noticed.

Again, it does not mean God literally counts the hairs on each person's head. It is a way of saying he knows each individual person very well.

● **Prayer/Reflection**
Hold up the number 6 billion on the roll of wallpaper again as you say the following prayer. Alternative: stop after line 3.

Six billion people
(pupils can draw faces in the naughts)
Six billion individuals
(pupils can invent and write names to go with the faces)
Always people, never just numbers.
Not one of them is forgotten by God.
Thank you, God, that you know each one of us,
Our names are written on your hand.

● **Music suggestions**
'God who made the earth', *Complete Come and Praise*, compiled by G. Marshall-Taylor (BBC, 1990)
'God knows me', *Complete Come and Praise*, compiled by G. Marshall-Taylor (BBC, 1990)
'I want to tell you', *Children's Praise*, compiled by P. Burt, P. Horrobin and G. Leavers (Marshall Pickering, 1991)

6 billion

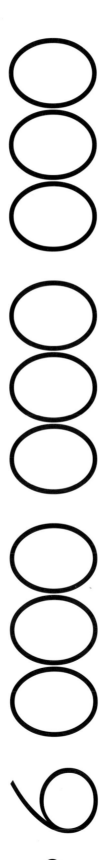

Symbolic numbers - 4

● Mathematical concepts
Working with whole numbers; counting up to 10 and beyond; count, sort and classify collections of objects; 3-D shapes and their properties: pyramid

● Numeracy Document links
Counting and recognising numbers
• Reception: count reliably up to 10 everyday objects
Solving problems
• Year 1: groups, sets
Measures, shape and space
• Year 2: use mathematical names for common 3-D shapes: ... pyramid; describe features

● Key Christian belief
The life of Jesus as Good News (Gospel)

● From the Bible
Matthew 5:16 (Paraphrase)
"Shine like a light so that people can see the good that you do and praise God."

Mark 4:35-40 (Paraphrase)
Jesus had been helping people all day and he was very tired, so he asked his disciples (friends) to sail to the other side of the lake while he slept in the back of the boat. While Jesus was sleeping a sudden storm broke and the boat was in danger of sinking, but Jesus was so tired that he slept through it. The disciples woke Jesus up. "Don't you care," they said. "We are about to drown!"
Jesus looked at them sadly, then turned to the wind and said. "Be Quiet!" and there was great calm.
The disciples were amazed. "Who is he?" they said. "Even the wind and waves obey him!"

Luke 15:1-4 (Paraphrase)
God is like a shepherd who cares for his sheep. Imagine a shepherd has one hundred sheep and loses one. He will leave the ninety nine in the pen and look for the one, lost sheep even though it means going by himself into the open country.

John 3:16 (Paraphrase)
"God loved the world so much that he sent us his only Son."

● You will need
Items in groups of 4
Paper and pens
Glue or stapler
Four candles in a baking tray of wet sand - optional

● Introduction
Note: *Italics = instructions for teachers*
Younger pupils: *Muddle up the items and ask pupils to put them in sets of four. Ask pupils to tell you about the number 4 (e.g. it is*

2x2, 3+1 etc.). Explain that today's assembly is about the number 4. Some numbers have special or symbolic meanings. We are going to learn about the number 4 and what it means to Christians.

Older pupils: *With help from the pupils, create a pyramid by taking a piece of A3 paper and gluing the two short edges together, creating a cylinder. Flatten the cylinder at one end and glue/ staple the edges together. Flatten it in the opposite direction (i.e. perpendicular to the way you flattened the other end) at the other end and glue/staple it. (**Note:** this may not immediately be recognisable as a pyramid - most pyramids are made up with equilateral triangles, this one is made up with isosceles triangles. It is the shape used by some manufacturers for pyramid teabags.) Ask pupils to examine the shape. How many sides does it have? (There are four sides.) The number four reminds Christians of four Bible writers.*

● Core material
All pupils: Matthew, Mark, Luke and John were people who gave their names to the four gospels *(books of the Bible). Ask how many of the pupils have these names.* The word 'gospel' just means 'good news'. *(See extra material on page 41.)*

Older pupils: *A person is a little like a shape with many sides (show the pyramid). Each gospel writer wrote about Jesus in a different way, emphasising a different side of Jesus' character. Read the biblical material and add a word/phrase to each side of the pyramid (see underlined words/phrases).*

Matthew tells the good news of Jesus the <u>teacher</u>.
Mark's good news is that Jesus was <u>powerful</u>.
Luke's good news is of Jesus the <u>carer</u>.
John's good news is that Jesus was really special. Christians believe he was <u>God's Son</u>.

Hold up the pyramid and show the words written on each side.

● Prayer/Reflection
Ask pupils to sit silently and think about a piece of good news they have heard recently.

Count to four (or place four candles in a tray of wet sand giving each candle the name of a gospel writer).

Just the number four, but it stands for four writers.
Thank you, Father, for all four gospels that tell us the good news. Life is often full of bad news but Matthew, Mark, Luke and John tell us the good news of Jesus.

● Music suggestions
'Come let us sing', *Junior Praise 1*, compiled by P. Horrobin and G. Leavers (Marshall Pickering, 1986)
'Mind the gap', *Kidsource*, compiled by A. Price (Kevin Mayhew, 1999)

How to make a pyramid

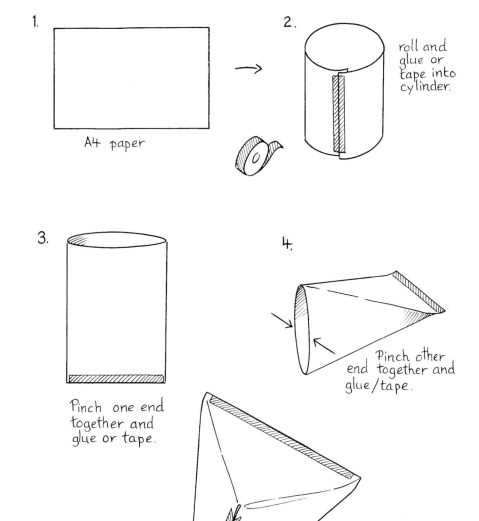

1. A4 paper

2. roll and glue or tape into cylinder.

3. Pinch one end together and glue or tape.

4. Pinch other end together and glue/tape.

5. Finished pyramid.

Alternative Core material for infants

*In the Core material, use only the paragraph marked **all pupils**. Ask one member of staff to come to the front and ask four people to say one thing (positive!) about her/him. (Arrange this beforehand.) The four statements should be different and show a different side of the person's character. Relate this to the way the gospel writers show four different sides of Jesus' character.*

Omit the readings if you think they will be too difficult for younger pupils. Ask them to think of good news they would like to hear. Explain that Matthew, Mark, Luke and John thought that Jesus was such good news that they wrote books about him.

41

Symbolic numbers – 7

● **Mathematical concepts**

Working with whole numbers; counting up to 10 and beyond; count, sort and classify collections of objects

● **Numeracy Document links**

Counting and recognising numbers
• Reception: count reliably up to 10 everyday objects
Solving problems
• Year 1: groups, sets

● **Key Christian belief**

Gifts of the Holy Spirit

● **From the Bible**

Romans 12:6-8 (CEV)

God has also given each of us different gifts. If our gift is to prophesy *(speak God's message)*, we should do it according to the amount of faith we have. If we can serve others, we should serve. If we can teach, we should teach. If we can encourage others, we should encourage them. If we can give, we should be generous. If we are leaders, we should do our best. If we are good to others, we should do it cheerfully.

● **You will need**

Items in groups of 7
Empty box, gift wrapped

● **Introduction**

Note: *Italics* = instructions for teachers

Muddle up the items (excluding the gift-wrapped box) and ask pupils (use infants if the assembly is mixed) to sort them into sets of seven. Ask pupils to tell you about 7 (3+4 etc.). Explain that today's assembly is about the number 7. Some numbers have special or symbolic meanings. We are going to learn about the number 7 and what it means to Christians.

This assembly is also about presents. *Show the pupils the present and ask them to guess what is inside. Ask them to open the present and show it to everyone else.* The box is empty because not every present can be gift wrapped. Today we are going to learn about seven invisible presents.

● **Core material**

For Christians, the number 7 is a special number, it reminds them of the Holy Spirit. The Holy Spirit is the name Christians give to God when he is a real but invisible friend. The Holy Spirit is also seen as the gift-giver. *Read the material from the Bible.* What the writer is asking people to do sounds very difficult, but in fact, it is quite easy. The writer says that people have different gifts or abilities given to them by God and people should use them for God and for others. The writer lists seven gifts: speaking God's message; serving; teaching; encouraging; giving; leading; kindness. *Write each of these seven gifts individually on a*

piece of paper. As you read the name of each gift and give the one line explanation, ask pupils to 'post' it into the box.

Explanation of the different gifts

1. SPEAKING: telling others God's message for the world.
2. SERVING: finding out what other people need and being willing to help them.
3. TEACHING: teaching people about God.
4. ENCOURAGING: praising people and helping them to do their best.
5. GIVING: sharing what you have with others.
6. LEADING: taking responsibility.
7. KINDNESS or being good to others: practical love in action.

Alternatives: write the different gifts on an enlarged version of the box (page 43);
using pupils, create tableux to demonstrate each 'gift';
use pictures (see page 43) to illustrate each 'gift'.

Christians believe that the Holy Spirit gives people some of these invisible gifts. One person may have the gift of teaching and be able to explain things clearly. Another person may have the gift of kindness and be able to give practical help to others. None of these gifts can be gift-wrapped or put in a box, but they are extremely valuable. When Christians see the number 7 it reminds them of these invisible gifts, the gifts of the Holy Spirit.

● **Prayer/Reflection**

Place the opened present on the table as a focus. Read the prayer below. Alternative: omit the third line.

Count to seven with the pupils.
Just a number, just seven;
A reminder of seven presents.
Thank you, Father, for invisible gifts.
They may not come in boxes.
They may not be wrapped,
But they are precious.

● **Music suggestions**

'Treasure all around', *Rejoice 1*, complied by A. White, A. Byrne and C. Malone (HarperCollins Religious, 1993)

'Presents', *Rejoice 1*, complied by A. White, A. Byrne and C. Malone (HarperCollins Religious, 1993)

'Make me a channel of your peace', *A Year of Celebration*, edited by J. Porter and J. McCrimmon (McCrimmon, 1995)

Speaking

Teaching

Giving

Serving

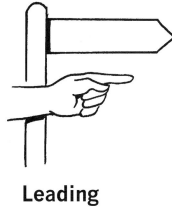

Leading

Kindness

Encouraging

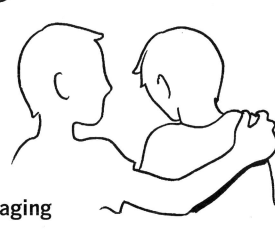

21

Symbolic numbers – 10

● Mathematical concepts

Working with whole numbers; counting up to 10 and beyond; count, sort and classify collections of objects

● Numeracy Document links

Counting and recognising numbers
• Reception: count reliably up to 10 everyday objects
Solving problems
• Year 1: groups, sets

● Key Christian belief

God's laws for living

● From the Bible

Deuteronomy 5:6-21 (GN)

"I am the LORD your God ... Worship no God but me.

"Do not make for yourselves idols ...

"Do not use my name for evil purposes ...

"Observe the <u>Sabbath</u> day *(the equivalent of Sunday for most Christians)* and keep it holy ... the seventh day is a day of rest ...

"Respect your father and your mother ...

"Do not commit murder.

"Do not commit <u>adultery</u> *(i.e. do not be unfaithful to your husband/wife).*

"Do not steal.

"Do not <u>accuse anyone falsely</u> *(tell lies about people).*

"Do not <u>desire</u> *(envy, be jealous of)* ... anything that belongs to your neighbour."

● You will need

Items in groups of 10
Enlarged copy of the island picture

● Introduction

Note: *Italics* = instructions for teachers

Muddle up the items and ask pupils to put them in sets of 10. Ask pupils to tell you about 10 (2x5 etc.). Explain that today's assembly is about the number 10. Some numbers have special or symbolic meanings. We are going to learn about the number 10 and what it means to Christians. The number 10 is easy to remember because we have 10 fingers *(or digits for **older pupils**)* and 10 toes. *They can count 1-10 on their own fingers.*

This assembly is also about rules or commandments. *Ask pupils to suggest some good rules for school and why they are needed.* If we each lived alone on a desert island, we would not need rules. If people live together, they need to agree on a way of behaving. *Some **older pupils** may have seen television programmes about groups of people living on islands and the difficulties that arose. You may wish to use the drawing of the desert island and ask pupils to draw up their own rules for living on the island. Use the picture of an island on page 45 as a stimulus.*

● Core material

Ten is a special number for Jews and Christians. It reminds them of God's 10 laws which are known as 'The Ten Commandments'. *Read the material from the Bible.* This can be put in easy language:

• Worship one God.
• No idols.
• Use God's name respectfully.
• Rest one day in each week.
• Respect your parents.
• Do not murder.
• Be faithful to your own husband or wife.
• Do not steal.
• Do not lie to get people into trouble.
• Do not be jealous of what other people have.

Write them up on a chart or board. These commandments were given to help people live at peace with God and each other. *Ask pupils to point out the ones that talk about God.* Which commandments help people live together? *Choose only one or two of the following examples for **younger pupils**. The incidents can be dramatised.*

• I keep wishing I had a car as good as my neighbor. I am very jealous of her. Which commandment am I breaking?
• I am in a shop, some sweets are very close and I take some. Which commandment am I breaking?
• I tell a lie when I am asked about an incident in the playground and an innocent person gets into trouble. Which commandment am I breaking?

● Prayer/Reflection

Use the prayer below. Alternative: ask pupils to think of a law, and think about what it allows, not what it stops. For example, 'No Stealing' allows people to enjoy their own property.

Count to 10 with the pupils.
Just a number, just 10,
A reminder of God's laws.
Thank you, Father, for your laws that help us live in peace with you and others.

● Music suggestions

'Father, lead me day by day', *Junior Praise 1*, compiled by P. Horrobin and G. Leavers (Marshall Pickering, 1986)
'Here I am, ready to go', *Kidsource*, compiled by A. Price (Kevin Mayhew, 1999)

Symbolic numbers – 12

● Mathematical concepts
Working with whole numbers; counting up to 10 and beyond; count, sort and classify collections of objects

● Numeracy Document links
Counting and recognising numbers
• Reception: count reliably up to 10 everyday objects
Solving problems
• Year 1: groups, sets
Numbers and the number system
• Year 1: count reliably at least 20 objects

● Key Christian belief
Following Jesus

● From the Bible
Mark 1:16-20 (GN)
As Jesus walked along the shore of Lake Galilee, he saw two fishermen, Simon and his brother Andrew, catching fish with a net. Jesus said to them, "Come with me and I will teach you to catch men." At once they left their nets and went with him. He went a little farther on and saw two other brothers, James and John, the sons of Zebedee. They were in their boat getting their nets ready. As soon as Jesus saw them he called them; they left their father Zebedee in the boat with the hired men and went with Jesus.

● You will need
12 pieces of paper or card and pens
Items in groups of 12
12 candles in a baking tray of wet sand
Matches
Sticky tack, scissors (optional)

● Introduction
Note: *Italics = instructions for teachers*
Muddle up the items and ask pupils to put them in sets of 12, or ask pupils to tell you about 12 (e.g. it is 4x3, 2x6 etc.). Explain that today's assembly is about the number 12. Some numbers have special or symbolic meanings. We are going to learn about the number 12 and what it means to Christians. Listen to the rhyme. How many of the names can you remember? *Write each name on a piece of card. Ask pupils if they know who these men were.*

Peter, Andrew, James and John
Were fishermen and disciples four.
Philip, Judas, James, Simon
Followed Jesus and made four more.
Ten was reached with Matthew and Thomas
Twelve complete with Nathaniel and Thaddaeus

● Core material
For Christians, the number 12 reminds them of the followers of Jesus (disciples). We are going to hear the story of how four of them followed Jesus. These four fishermen already knew Jesus

so that when he called them to follow him, they knew they were following someone they could trust. *Read the material from the Bible.* We know a little about some of these disciples. *Choose 12 pupils to act as the disciples. Give each pupil one of the disciple name cards. Introduce each 'disciple' to the rest of the assembly and add some information about them.*

First of all, I would like to introduce the four fishermen:
  Simon-Peter
  Andrew
  James and John.

Now I would like to introduce two friends:
  Philip and Nathaniel.

There are two disciples we know little about, only their names:
  Thaddaeus and James the Younger.

The final four are:
  Matthew the tax collector
  Simon the Patriot
  Judas the betrayer
  Thomas the doubter.

The disciples were all very different and none of them were perfect. Many were quite ordinary. It is the same with Jesus' followers today.

● Prayer/Reflection
Place the 12 candles in the damp sand. As you light each candle, say the name of one disciple and say something about that person: "Peter the fisherman" etc. and ask pupils to think about them. Alternative: photocopy the picture onto paper and cut it into strips, each strip showing one candle. Ask pupils to stick the strips to the wall one at the time, as each name is read out (as if putting together a jigsaw). Alternative: photocopy the picture onto an acetate and cover the candles with a sheet of paper, reveal the candles one at a time.

Thank you, Lord, for all your followers, famous and ordinary. Thank you that they were not perfect but that did not stop you from choosing them.

● Music suggestions
'Jesus went a-walking', *Many Ways to Praise*, by S. Sayers (Kevin Mayhew, 1986)
'We're following Jesus', *Junior Praise 2*, compiled by P. Burt, P. Horrobin and G. Leavers (Marshall Pickering, 1992)

Peter
Andrew
James
John
Philip
Judas
James
Simon
Matthew
Thomas
Nathaniel
Thaddeus

A S S E M B L I E S   T H A T   C O U N T

Resouces to count on!

The Stapleford Centre supports teachers with a wide variety of resources for teaching Christianity in the Primary curriculum. Apart from *Assemblies that Count*, The Stapleford Centre offers:

- a range of other resource books for assemblies
- a wide variety of teacher's resources for teaching Christianity in RE
- resources to encourage spiritual and moral development in other subjects in the Primary curriculum
- *CRACKING RE* · a photocopiable termly resource for Primary RE and assembly

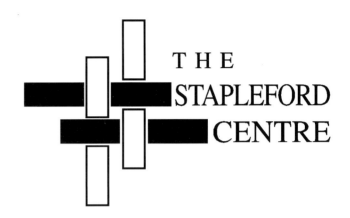

THE **STAPLEFORD CENTRE**

- INSET for RE and assembly, e.g. *Using the Bible in Literacy Teaching*
- Distance learning courses in RE to Certificate, Diploma and MA levels, validated by the University of Nottingham.

For information about subscribing to *CRACKING RE*, and for details of all other resources and training courses available from The Stapleford Centre, photocopy and complete this form, PRINTING the information. Then fax or post the form to The Stapleford Centre.

Please send me details about:

☐ Subscribing to *CRACKING RE*

☐ Other Primary school resources published by The Stapleford Centre

☐ Courses for Primary teachers run by The Stapleford Centre

Name: _____ E-mail: _____

Address _____

Postcode: _____

Telephone: _____ Fax: _____

Photocopy, complete, then fax or post to:

The Stapleford Centre
The Old Lace Mill
Frederick Road, Stapleford
Nottingham NG9 8FN

Telephone: 0115 939 6270
Fax: 0115 939 2076
E-mail: admin@stapleford-centre.org
Web site: www.stapleford-centre.org

www.stapleford-centre.org

Visit our web site to see other resources available for Primary school RE, assemblies and other subjects in the Primary curriculum including literacy teaching. Order your resources on-line!

Registered office: The Stapleford Centre, The Old Lace Mill, Frederick Road, Stapleford, Nottingham NG9 8FN
A company limited by guarantee, registered in England and Wales, number 3771977
Registered Charity number 1063856   VAT number 695 1265 12